mochi, cakes and bakes

Simple Yet Exquisite Desserts with Ube, Yuzu, Matcha and More

catherine zhang

winner of Netflix's *Zumbo's Just Desserts* season 2

PAGE STREET
PUBLISHING CO.

First published in 2022 by

Page Street Publishing Co.

27 Congress Street, Suite 1511

Salem, MA 01970

www.pagestreetpublishing.com

Distributed by Macmillan, sales in Canada by The Canadian Manda Group.

26   25   24   23   22   1   2   3   4   5

ISBN-13: 978-1-64567-636-2

ISBN-10: 1-64567-636-6

Library of Congress Control Number: 2022935161

Cover and book design by Katie Beasley for Page Street Publishing Co.

Photography by Catherine Zhang

Printed and bound in China

dedication

To everyone working toward their dreams.

contents

foreword by adriano zumbo

I first met Catherine on the set of *Zumbo's Just Desserts,* and she was a shy young lady just fresh from school, trying to find her way in the baking competition. I quickly came to realize that she had some great skills and talent in dessert making as she slowly started to bring some flair and finesse to her creations. Flavor and texture are the first things I teach to anyone looking to up their game in memorable desserts and creations. And these are things that Catherine really had strengths in.

We are now many years on from that first connection and experience in dessert pressure and craziness.

It has been wonderful to watch Catherine's skills and confidence grow over the years, from her recipe development career to her blog and now with writing her new book.

Catherine has grown from strength to strength, from standing in front of crowds to filming teaching videos with that natural ability to connect with her followers, fans and fellow bakers who share her burning passion.

Catherine is bringing out a new style and creative direction that stems from her Asian heritage and imaginative flair, encompassing bold and balanced Asian flavors and textures, and blending them with some of the world's different cultural dessert staples.

I have no doubt that this book will be spectacular and deserving of a place on the shelves of an avid dessert lover or any adventurous home cook or chef.

introduction

I'm an Australian-born Chinese who loves to bake, and I'd like to think of this book as a representation of me in the form of delicious recipes and Asian-inspired treats.

Growing up I was the only foodie in the household. Yes, the rest of my family enjoyed food, but cooking and entertaining were never their strong points. I, on the other hand, was obsessed with food, and so from an early age, I decided that it would be my role. Whether it was cooking up Sunday brunch, a birthday cake or Christmas dinner, I wanted to be the one who brought delicious food and smiles to my family and friends' faces.

Throughout primary and high school, cooking was my escape, and there's something about baking that is so therapeutic. On top of that, there is so much creative potential when making desserts, whether decorating cookies or icing a cake. And that's what made me fall in love with desserts.

Knowing my love for food, I decided to choose a career in food science and nutrition with the ultimate goal of becoming a dietitian. Looking at the number of desserts I eat these days, it was a funny career choice, but one that nonetheless has helped me on the path I'm on now.

I was halfway through my university degree when I decided to take my mum and check out a dessert expo. Why? Just because I wanted to eat some cake and hoard baking supplies. Instead, I was met with an opportunity to apply for a competitive baking show. I was against applying because I thought I wouldn't stand a chance, but my mum thought it would be a great idea and convinced me to give it a shot. To my surprise, after a couple rounds of auditions, I was given the opportunity to appear on season two of *Zumbo's Just Desserts*!

Never in a million years did I think I would get the chance to appear on national and worldwide television, let alone cook for my idol, Adriano Zumbo. It was a crazy experience. I met some of the most passionate and wonderful people, created some of the craziest desserts and won . . . I remember every single second of it and am forever grateful for the opportunity. I emerged stronger and more passionate about desserts than ever. I also knew I needed to bake.

The path to where I am now hasn't been an easy one. Whether I was working as a pastry chef, operating my own small business or starting a baking blog, I've had my ups and downs, but I also found a stronger understanding of my purpose and passion. Now I'm working as a recipe developer, while my blog and online platform continues to grow. And hey, who knew I'd be writing, styling and shooting my very own cookbook!

As I continue to bake, I've realized my palate tends toward the flavors I'm familiar with, the ones I've grown up eating and loving. Australia is such a multicultural country, and I am blessed to be surrounded by cultures from all over the world through friends and coworkers, restaurants and shops and events and activities.

However, despite the cultural diversity in Australia, growing up I found myself largely surrounded by the East Asian community. My closest friends were of Chinese, Japanese and South Korean ancestry, and I was constantly learning new parts of their cultures and cuisines. I studied Japanese for six years, and I studied in South Korea during university. My first job was in a sushi restaurant owned by the sweetest South Korean couple, and I spent a large portion of time working in a modern Cantonese restaurant.

While I may be Australian on paper, at heart, I'm made up of all the cultures and experiences of the people who shaped me. I grew up enjoying the flavors in this book, and I wanted to share them with the world in the form of delicious desserts.

I won *Zumbo's Just Desserts* at nineteen and am publishing my own cookbook at twenty-three. I know this is only the beginning of a long, long journey, and I can't wait to see where life will take me. At this age, life is full of opportunities, and all we need to do is work toward them! I'm still as confused as I was fresh out of university, just with a little more experience under my belt, but I hope I can inspire and provide you with a collection of desserts you'll be making over and over again.

As much as baking is fun and delicious, it's also a science. As a food science major, I love diving into the smaller details of baking to perfect each element. That being said, I've done all the hard work, and all you need to do is bake and learn. While the measurements throughout the book are both imperial and metric, I highly recommend using a kitchen scale to weigh out your ingredients to ensure baking success!

From traditional treats like Hong Kong Egg Tarts (page 116) and mochi (page 24) to completely new adaptations of classic desserts like Black Sesame Praline Macarons (page 98) and Raspberry Yuzu Cream Puffs (page 119), let me take you on a journey through a new world of Asian-inspired sweets.

Catherine xx

the essentials

Every baker should be equipped with a strong set of basic recipes they can fall back on. These are the perfected versions of my very best recipes. They have never let me down and will become the foundation for not only the recipes in this book but the desserts that you will create in the future!

The essentials I like to keep in my back pocket are the Cotton-Soft Sponge Cake Base (page 19), Sweet Shortcrust Tart Pastry (page 11), Milk Bun Base (page 23), Pastry Cream (page 20) and a couple of buttercreams and ganaches. With just a few solid basics, the different dessert combinations you can create are endless. Use this chapter to build your very own set of essential recipes that you can use and adapt in your own baking. All you need to do is switch up the flavors with a dusting of cocoa, a splash of fruit and a touch of creativity!

sweet shortcrust tart pastry

Sweet tart pastry, *pâte sablée* in French, is a versatile base for any kind of sweet tart. This pastry is sweet and buttery with a crisp and slightly short texture. If you're looking for a basic but sturdy tart shell, this is the one! I've baked these in tart rings for a classic French-patisserie-style tartlet, but feel free to use a regular tart tin or tartlet tins.

makes 12 (3-inch [8-cm]) tartlet shells

2 cups (240 g) all-purpose flour

¾ cup + 1 tbsp (100 g) powdered sugar

⅓ cup (32 g) almond meal

Pinch of salt

½ cup (120 g) unsalted butter, chilled, cubed

1 large egg, beaten

Baking beans or uncooked rice, for filling the shells

In a large bowl, combine the flour, powdered sugar, almond meal, salt and butter, and use your fingertips to rub the butter into the flour until it resembles sand. Add the egg and mix until a shaggy dough forms. Transfer the dough to a floured surface and form it into a ball.

Feel free to use a food processor for a quick, fuss-free dough. Simply pulse the flour, sugar, almond meal, salt and butter until a fine crumb forms before streaming in the egg to form a shaggy dough.

Divide the dough in half and roll each half out between two sheets of baking paper to 2 mm in thickness. Transfer the rolled sheets of dough to a baking tray and chill for 1 hour, or until firm.

Once the dough has chilled, line a baking tray with baking paper. Place twelve 3-inch (8-cm) tart rings on the baking tray. Remove the baking paper from the chilled dough and cut out twelve 3-inch (8-cm) dough circles. Line the base of the tart rings with the dough circles. Using a ruler, cut out strips of dough slightly wider than the height of your tart rings and line the sides of the rings. Trim the excess dough, dock the base with a fork and chill for 1 hour, or until firm.

To bake the tart shells, preheat the oven to 350°F (180°C). Prepare the chilled tart shells for blind baking by lining the insides with baking paper and filling them with baking beans or uncooked rice. Blind bake for 15 minutes, then remove the beans or rice and bake for a further 5 to 10 minutes until golden brown. Remove from the oven and cool for 1 hour, or until completely cooled before removing the tart rings.

french macaron shells

Macarons are cookies that have come with me on a long and difficult journey. I think it's safe to say I've come a long way from the cracked and lopsided macarons I made ten years ago. These macaron shells are made using a French meringue base for a quick and easy shell without the sticky mess of making a sugar syrup. For precision, make sure you weigh out your ingredients to ensure macaron perfection. Macarons may be finicky to make at first, but once you nail the method, you'll be making perfect shells every time!

makes 18 filled macarons

¾ cup + 1 tbsp (80 g) almond meal

⅔ cup (75 g) powdered sugar

1 tsp white vinegar or lemon juice

4 tbsp (60 g) egg whites, approx. 2 large egg whites

¼ cup + 1 tbsp (60 g) granulated sugar

Gel or powdered food coloring, optional

Sieve the almond meal and powdered sugar together into a bowl, discarding any large chunks of almond meal that don't pass through the sieve. This ensures the shells are smooth.

Soak a paper towel with the white vinegar, and wipe down the bowl of a stand mixer before adding the egg whites. This helps the egg whites whip up to a stable meringue. Fix the bowl to a stand mixer fitted with a whisk attachment and whisk on medium speed for 2 minutes, or until the egg whites are foamy. Add the granulated sugar and whisk on high speed for 5 minutes, or until the meringue forms stiff peaks. At this point, you can add food coloring if using and whisk until well combined [1].

Fold the sieved almond meal and powdered sugar into the meringue with a rubber spatula in two additions, scraping around the bowl and down the center to combine. Once the mixture is just combined, spread the batter along the inside surface of the bowl and back into the center. Continue to spread and fold the batter until the batter falls back into the bowl as a slow ribbon. The lines that form when the batter falls back into the bowl should almost meld into the batter after 20 seconds.

Folding the batter to the right consistency is key to creating the perfect macaron shell. Fold slowly and check the consistency as you go [2]. Over-mixing the batter can lead to flat macarons, while undermixed batter can lead to cracks. When in doubt, stop mixing and check!

Once the right consistency has been reached, transfer the batter to a piping bag fitted with a medium-sized round piping tip. Pipe 1.5-inch (3.5-cm) circles onto a large baking tray lined with baking paper, leaving 1 inch (2.5 cm) in between to prevent them from spreading into each other.

Leave the trays of piped macarons, uncovered, on the countertop to dry for 1 to 2 hours, or until the surface of the shell is matte and dry. You should be able to touch the surface of the shell without it sticking to your finger [3].

To bake the shells, preheat the oven to 285°F (140°C) and bake the dried shells for 14 to 16 minutes until the macarons don't shift when wiggled. Remove from the oven and cool for 1 hour, or until completely cooled, before filling [4].

almond tart pastry

This pastry makes a shorter, crumblier tart base with an addictive nutty flavor. The high butter percentage gives it a melt-in-your-mouth texture, but also makes it fragile and prone to breakage. Pair this tart pastry with sturdy fillings that will give it more structure, like caramels or ganaches.

makes 6 (3-inch [8-cm]) tartlets or 1 (9.5-inch [24-cm]) round tart

1½ cups (180 g) all-purpose flour

¾ cup (75 g) almond meal

2 tbsp (25 g) granulated sugar

⅔ cup (150 g) unsalted butter, chilled, cubed

1 tbsp (15 ml) water, iced

Baking beans or uncooked riced, for blind baking

To make the almond tart dough, combine the flour, almond meal and sugar in a large bowl and use your fingertips to rub the butter into the flour until it resembles sand. Add the water and mix until a shaggy dough forms. Transfer the dough to a floured surface and form it into a ball [1].

Feel free to use a food processor for a quick, fuss-free dough. Simply pulse the flour, almond meal, sugar and butter until a fine crumb forms before streaming in the water to form a shaggy dough.

To make tartlets, roll the dough [2] out between two sheets of baking paper to 2 mm in thickness [3]. Transfer the rolled sheet of dough to a baking tray and chill for 1 hour, or until firm. Once chilled, remove the baking paper and use a cookie cutter slightly larger than the diameter of your tartlet tins to cut rounds from the chilled dough. Using your fingers, carefully press the dough into the tartlet tins [4], then fold and press the overhanging edges of dough against the edges of the tins to trim the edges of the dough. Once the tins are lined, dock the bases with a fork. Chill for 30 minutes, or until firm.

To make a 9.5-inch (24-cm) tart, place the dough on top of a large sheet of baking paper and top with a similar-sized piece of cling wrap. Using a rolling pin, roll the dough out to a 3-mm-thick circle [3]. Flip the dough and remove the piece of baking paper, then carefully line the tart tin with the dough, cling-wrapped side facing up. Using your fingers, carefully press the dough into the tin [4], then fold and press the overhanging edge of dough against the edge of the tin to trim the edges of the dough. Once the tin is lined, carefully remove the cling wrap and dock the base with a fork. Chill for 1 hour, or until firm.

To bake the tart shell or shells, preheat the oven to 350°F (180°C). Prepare the chilled tart shell or shells for blind baking by lining the insides with baking paper and filling with baking beans or uncooked rice [5]. Bake the tart for 45 minutes or the tartlets for 30 minutes. Then remove the beans or rice and bake for a further 5 to 10 minutes, until golden brown. If the edges begin to burn, but the base is still pale, cover the edges with aluminum foil and continue to bake the tart until the base is golden brown [6].

roll cake base

Roll cakes are a classic in all Asian bakeries, and I grew up eating these soft and fluffy cakes filled with whipped cream. This roll cake is super versatile and can be adjusted according to your favorite flavor. Feel free to play around with fillings; from jam to whipped cream, buttercream, fresh fruit and even your favorite spreads, the options are endless.

makes 1 roll cake base

3 tbsp (45 ml) whole milk

4 large eggs, yolks and whites separated

3 tbsp + 1 tsp (50 ml) vegetable oil

¼ cup + 2 tbsp (75 g) granulated sugar, divided

¾ cup (85 g) cake flour

Preheat the oven to 320°F (160°C) and line a 9 x 13-inch (22 x 33-cm) rectangular pan with baking paper.

In a small saucepan over medium heat, heat the milk for 3 minutes, or until steaming. Meanwhile, in a medium-sized heatproof bowl, combine the egg yolks, oil and 2 tablespoons (25 g) of sugar [1], and whisk to combine. Slowly pour the steaming milk into the egg yolk mixture, whisking continuously until well combined. Sieve the cake flour into the egg yolk mixture and whisk until smooth and just combined [2].

In the bowl of a stand mixer fitted with a whisk attachment, add the egg whites and beat on medium-high speed for 3 minutes, or until the egg whites are foamy with soft peaks [3]. Add the remaining ¼ cup (50 g) of sugar and continue to whisk for 5 minutes, or until the meringue forms stiff peaks. Fold one-third of the meringue into the egg yolk mixture and whisk until smooth [4]. Add the lightened egg yolk mixture to the remaining meringue and carefully fold the batter until just combined [5]. Slowly pour the batter into the lined tin [6] and bake for 25 minutes or until the cake springs back when touched [7].

In order to form a perfect shape when filled, it is important to roll the cake before it cools. This sets the cake's final shape and prevents cracks when filling. Working quickly, flip the just-baked cake onto a clean sheet of baking paper. Remove the piece of baking paper attached to the cake and replace it with a clean kitchen towel. Flip the cake so the kitchen towel is on the bottom and roll the cake from one short end to the other [8]. The kitchen towel should be on the outside and the baking paper should be on the inside. Continue to roll until a log forms and place the roll seam side down in the fridge to chill for 1 hour, or until completely cooled [9].

To make a Matcha Roll Cake: Replace 1 tablespoon (10 g) of cake flour with 1 tablespoon (6 g) of matcha powder.

To make a Chocolate Roll Cake: Replace 2 tablespoons (20 g) of cake flour with 2 tablespoons (10 g) of cocoa powder.

To make an Ube Roll Cake: Add 1 teaspoon of ube extract to the egg yolk mixture before folding with the meringue.

cotton-soft sponge cake base

The characteristic dessert of any Asian bakery is a sponge cake so soft it feels like you are eating a cloud. I've been on the hunt for the perfect cotton-soft sponge cake ever since the beginning of my baking journey and this sponge cake will not disappoint. Best served with light whipped cream, this is the cake you'll be making over and over again.

makes 1 (6-inch [15-cm]) or 1 (8-inch [20-cm]) cake

6-inch (15-cm) cake

3 large eggs, yolks and whites separated

3 tbsp (45 ml) whole milk

2 tbsp + 1 tsp (35 ml) vegetable oil

⅓ cup (40 g) cornstarch

⅓ cup (40 g) all-purpose flour

⅓ cup (65 g) granulated sugar

8-inch (20-cm) cake

4 large eggs, yolks and whites separated

¼ cup (60 ml) whole milk

3 tbsp (45 ml) vegetable oil

⅓ cup + 2 tbsp (55 g) cornstarch

⅓ cup + 2 tbsp (55 g) all-purpose flour

⅓ cup + 2 tbsp (90 g) granulated sugar

Preheat the oven to 300°F (150°C). Line the base of a 6-inch (15-cm) or 8-inch (20-cm) cake tin with baking paper. There is no need to grease the sides of the pan, as the sides will act as a wall on which the cake batter can climb. This results in a taller and fluffier cake.

In a medium-sized mixing bowl, combine the egg yolks, milk and oil, and whisk until combined [1]. Add the cornstarch and whisk until smooth and well combined. Sieve in the flour, whisk until just combined and set aside [2].

Add the egg whites to the bowl of a stand mixer fitted with a whisk attachment and whisk on medium-high speed for 2 minutes, or until the egg whites are foamy. Add the sugar and continue to whisk for 5 minutes, or until the meringue forms stiff peaks. Fold one-third of the meringue into the egg yolk mixture and whisk until smooth [3]. Transfer the lightened egg yolk mixture to the remaining meringue and carefully fold the batter until just combined [4]. Slowly pour the batter into the lined tin, tap lightly to level off the surface and place in a large baking tray filled with ½-inch (1-cm) of hot, but not boiling, water.

Bake the 6-inch (15-cm) cake for 1 hour or the 8-inch (20-cm) cake for 1 hour and 10 minutes, until the cake springs back when touched [5]. Remove the cake from the oven and cool for 1 hour, or until completely cooled. The cake should level off as it cools. Don't worry if the cake is cracked on top; this can be trimmed and the sponge cake below will be pillowy soft.

Once cooled, run a thin knife along the edge of the pan to release the sides. Invert the pan to unmold the cake and remove the attached baking paper [6]. Wrap the cake in cling wrap and chill!

To make a Matcha Sponge Cake: For a 6-inch (15-cm) cake, replace 1 tablespoon (8 g) of flour with 1 tablespoon (6 g) of matcha powder. For an 8-inch (20-cm) cake, replace 2 tablespoons (20 g) of flour with 2 tablespoons (12 g) of matcha powder.

To make a Chocolate Sponge Cake: For a 6-inch (15-cm) cake, replace 1 tablespoon (8 g) of flour with 1 tablespoon (5 g) of cocoa powder. For an 8-inch (20-cm) cake, replace 2 tablespoons (20 g) of flour with 2 tablespoons (10 g) of cocoa powder.

pastry cream

Pastry cream, *crème pâtissière* in French, is a staple in baking. Whether it's in a fruit flan, cake, profiterole or Danish, there is always a place for a creamy custard. Traditionally, pastry cream is prepared with all-purpose flour. However, flour has a tendency to clump up and create a lumpy custard. Using cornstarch produces a creamy and silky-smooth consistency every time!

makes 1 cup (240 ml) pastry cream

1 cup (240 ml) whole milk

3 large egg yolks

⅓ cup (65 g) granulated sugar

3 tbsp (22 g) cornstarch

1 tsp vanilla extract

2 tbsp (30 g) unsalted butter

In a medium saucepan over medium heat, heat the milk for 3 minutes, or until it's steaming [1]. Meanwhile, in a medium-sized heatproof bowl, combine the egg yolks, sugar, cornstarch and vanilla extract, and whisk until combined [2]. Slowly pour the steaming milk into the egg yolks, whisking continuously until well combined [3]. Return the custard mixture to the saucepan and whisk over medium heat for 3 to 4 minutes, or until thickened. It should be thick enough to hold a line when a utensil is drawn across the base of the saucepan [4].

Remove the custard from the heat and add the butter, stirring until melted [5]. Transfer to a medium-sized bowl and cover with cling wrap. Ensure the cling wrap is touching the surface of the pastry cream to prevent the cream from developing a film [6]. Chill for 1 to 2 hours, or until completely cooled, before using.

milk bun base

One of the best feelings is sinking your teeth into a soft, light and fragrant bread roll. Asian bakery bread has that characteristic sweet and milky flavor with a super light texture that isn't usually found in Western bakeries. This milk bun base dough is the perfect recreation of my childhood and works with any filling, savory or sweet.

makes 10 milk buns

water roux

3 tbsp (24 g) bread flour

½ cup (120 ml) water

dough

2¾ cups (380 g) bread flour

¾ cup (90 g) all-purpose flour

¼ cup (27 g) milk powder

⅓ cup + 1 tbsp (78 g) granulated sugar

¾ tsp salt

2¼ tsp (7 g) instant dry yeast

1 large egg, lightly beaten

⅔ cup (160 ml) water, lukewarm

3 tbsp (45 g) unsalted butter, softened, cubed

glaze

1 large egg

1 tbsp (15 ml) whole milk

To make the water roux, combine the bread flour and water [1] in a small saucepan. Whisk over medium heat for 5 minutes, or until thickened and semi-translucent [2]. Remove from the heat and transfer to a bowl. Cover with cling wrap and cool for 1 hour, or until room temperature before use.

To make the dough, combine the bread flour, all-purpose flour, milk powder, sugar, salt and yeast [3] in the bowl of a stand mixer fitted with a dough hook. Add the egg, water and cooled roux and mix on medium for 3 minutes, or until a rough dough forms. Ensure the added water is at 99°F (37°C), the same temperature as your body.

Add the butter and continue to knead on medium for 20 minutes [4], or until the dough passes the windowpane test (at this stage, the dough can be stretched into a thin sheet that resembles a windowpane without tearing).

Roll the dough into a ball and place it in a large bowl greased with oil for the first proof. Loosely cover with cling wrap and place in a warm place for 1 to 2 hours, or until doubled in size [5]. A turned-off oven with a mug of hot water is a warm and moist environment perfect for proofing. The dough is ready when a floured finger inserted into the center creates a hole that doesn't bounce back [6].

After the first proof, the dough is ready to be shaped and used in any recipe, or shaped and baked as plain milk buns.

To make milk buns, transfer the dough to a lightly floured surface and gently press out the air. Divide the dough into ten equal portions, roll into balls and place on a tray. Cover with cling wrap and place the tray in a warm place for 1 hour, or until doubled in size.

Meanwhile, preheat the oven to 375°F (190°C). Make the glaze by whisking the egg and milk together. Once the bread has finished proofing, brush it with the glaze. Bake for 12 to 15 minutes until golden brown, then cool for 15 minutes before enjoying.

mochi base

This is a simple mochi base recipe that is sweet, chewy and delicious! Mochi are super versatile and can be paired with whatever filling you desire for a bouncy treat. Microwave the batter for a quick fix or steam it for an even and consistent texture.

makes approx. 8 to 10 mochi

1 cup (130 g) glutinous rice flour

¼ cup (50 g) granulated sugar

¼ cup (30 g) cornstarch

1 cup (240 ml) water or other liquid as specified in recipe

1 tbsp (15 ml) vegetable oil

In a large heatproof bowl, combine the glutinous rice flour, sugar, cornstarch and water [1]. Whisk until combined [2].

To microwave the mochi, cover the bowl with cling wrap and use a fork to pierce several holes [3]. This allows built-up steam to escape while cooking. Microwave on high for 2 minutes before removing and mixing to incorporate any raw areas of dough [4]. Re-cover the bowl and microwave in 1-minute intervals until the mochi dough is semi-translucent and no longer milky. This should take a total of 3 to 4 minutes. Keep covered and cool for 15 minutes, or until cooled enough to touch.

To steam the mochi, place a steamer over boiling water and transfer the batter to a shallow heatproof bowl. Cover with cling wrap and steam for 30 to 40 minutes, or until the mochi dough is semi-translucent and no longer milky. Keep covered and cool for 15 minutes, or until cooled enough to touch.

Once the mochi has cooled sufficiently, add the oil. Using gloved or oiled hands [5], knead the cooled mochi dough until smooth and stretchy. Kneading the dough helps incorporate the oil while enhancing the mochi's chewy texture.

The mochi is now ready to be shaped and filled [6], or eaten plain dusted with powders like cornstarch, soybean or peanut powder.

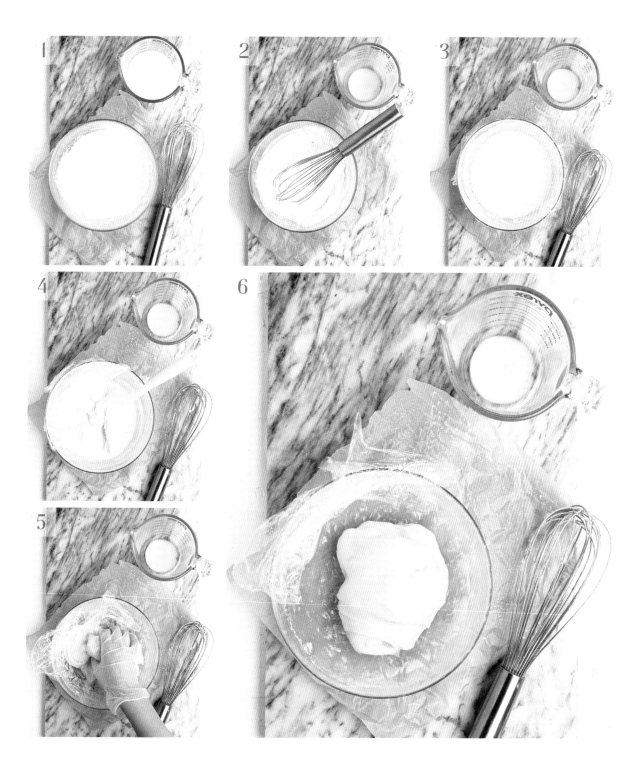

all things mochi

Sweetened glutinous rice cakes, most commonly known by their Japanese name mochi (餅), are soft and chewy treats made from glutinous rice. While the Japanese name "mochi" has been popularized worldwide, this delicious treat goes by many different names in countries all across Asia such as chapssaltteok (찹쌀떡) in South Korea and lo mai chi (糯米糍) in China. Each country's version has its own unique flavor profile and preparation method with variations that go beyond a simple, filled rice cake.

Coming from a Chinese background, I grew up eating delicious treats made from glutinous rice flour like zhīmáqíu (芝麻球) or tāngyuán (汤圆). The first is a deep-fried sesame ball commonly filled with red bean paste and the latter is a boiled glutinous rice dumpling that can contain all kinds of fillings ranging from black sesame to peanut butter!

Asian cuisine is becoming more popular, and these treats I savored in the comfort of my own home are now widely enjoyed across the world. The resulting fusion of Eastern and Western flavors gives a whole new meaning to these chewy rice treats. This chapter will take you on a journey through traditional mochi like Japan's ichigo daifuku (大福), or Strawberry Mochi (page 32), and new takes on classics like zhīmáqíu (芝麻球) with Molten Salted Egg Sesame Balls (page 40) to the ultimate fusion of cultures in treats like Cookies and Cream Snow Skin Mooncakes (page 44).

mochi donuts

Originating in Japan's most well-known donut store, Mister Donut, this mochi donut, or pon de ring (ポンデリング), is a glazed donut with a mochi-like texture. While they may be called mochi donuts, the batter itself doesn't contain any glutinous rice flour and instead uses tapioca starch to create a mochi-like texture. The best thing about this recipe is its versatility. Customize these donuts as you like by baking or frying, adding different flavorings and toppings or keeping it simple with just a glaze. When fried, the donuts are a little crispier and more fragrant, while baking removes the hassle of deep-frying for an equally delicious chewy donut.

makes 10 donuts

donuts

⅓ cup + 1 tbsp (95 ml) whole milk

2 tbsp + 1 tsp (30 g) granulated sugar

1 tbsp + 2 tsp (25 ml) vegetable oil

2 tbsp + 2 tsp (20 g) all-purpose flour

¾ cup (90 g) tapioca starch

1 large egg, beaten

Vegetable oil, to fry, optional

glaze

¾ cup + 1 tbsp (100 g) powdered sugar

2 tsp (4 g) matcha powder, optional

2 tbsp (12 g) freeze-dried strawberry powder, optional

2 tbsp (30 ml) whole milk

Crushed biscuits or sprinkles, optional

To make the donuts, line a baking tray with baking paper. Using a pencil, trace ten circles on the underside of the baking paper using a 2.5-inch (6-cm) cookie cutter.

Heat the milk, sugar and oil in a small saucepan for 4 minutes, or until just boiling. Remove from the heat and sieve in the flour and tapioca starch. Mix until smooth and completely combined. The batter should resemble a thick paste. Transfer the dough to a large bowl and slowly add the egg. Continue to add the egg until the batter is thin enough to hang from the spatula, but not so thin that it falls off the spatula in ribbons. Transfer the batter to a piping bag fitted with a medium-sized round tip. Pipe six equally spaced mounds around the circumference of one traced circle, ensuring the mounds are just touching each other. Repeat with the remaining traced circles.

To fry the donuts, heat a heavy-bottomed pot of vegetable oil, or a deep fryer, to 320°F (160°C). Cut the baking paper so that each piped donut is on its own piece of paper. Drop two to three donuts into the hot oil at a time, removing the baking paper after 30 seconds. Fry the donuts for 1 to 2 minutes on each side, or until a deep golden brown. Remove from the oil, drain on a wire rack or paper towel and cool for 30 minutes or until completely cooled. To bake the donuts, preheat the oven to 340°F (170°) and bake the piped donuts for 13 to 15 minutes, or until golden brown. Remove from the oven and cool for 30 minutes or until completely cooled.

To make the glaze, combine the powdered sugar and your flavoring of choice, if using, in a small bowl and whisk until combined. Add 2 teaspoons (10 ml) of milk at a time, mixing in between each addition until the glaze feels thick, but falls back into the bowl in ribbons. Dip the cooled donuts into the glaze and carefully lift them to remove. Allow the excess glaze to drip off before turning the donut glaze side up and placing it on a wire rack to set for an hour. Repeat with the remaining donuts and decorate with crushed biscuits, if using.

These are best enjoyed on the day they're made, as tapioca starch will firm up over time. If they get a little stale, place them in the microwave for 10 seconds or so to soften.

mango coconut mochi

Coconut mochi, or glutinous rice dumpling, is called nuòmǐcí (糯米糍) in Mandarin or luo mai chi in Cantonese. It is a staple in any Chinese bakery. Originating in Hong Kong and the Guangdong province of China, these can be filled with anything from a classic sweetened red bean paste to one of my personal favorites, mango!

makes 10 mochi

coconut mochi

1 batch Mochi Base (page 24)

½ cup (120 ml) whole milk and ½ cup (120 ml) coconut milk

assembly

1 cup (95 g) desiccated coconut, for rolling

2 large mangoes, cut into 0.8-inch (2-cm) cubes

Prepare the mochi dough as per the Mochi Base recipe (page 24), using the milk and coconut milk combination instead of water. Cool for 30 minutes or until completely cooled.

To assemble, place the coconut in a shallow bowl. Wear food-safe gloves greased with vegetable oil. This prevents the mochi from sticking to your hands while keeping the mochi tacky enough to enclose the filling. Line a baking tray with baking paper. Divide the mochi into ten equal balls and place them on the prepared tray. Flatten each ball in between your palms and place a cube of mango in the center. Bring the edges of the mochi together to enclose the mango, then pinch to seal and roll in the coconut. Repeat until all the mochi balls have been used.

These are best enjoyed the day they're made as mochi firms up over time. Store any remaining mochi in an airtight container at room temperature for up to 2 days.

strawberry mochi

Strawberry mochi, or ichigo daifuku (いちご大福), are a classic wagashi (和菓子), or Japanese confection. They are most commonly found in the springtime when fresh seasonal strawberries are available. The term daifuku (大福) describes a filled mochi, typically with red bean paste, and the word ichigo (いちご) means strawberry. Together they create a perfectly balanced treat!

makes 10 mochi

red bean paste

½ cup (100 g) adzuki (red) beans

Water, to cover the beans

½ cup (90 g) brown sugar, unpacked

1 tbsp (15 ml) vegetable oil

mochi base

1 batch Mochi Base (page 24)

1 cup (240 ml) whole milk

assembly

10 whole strawberries

Cornstarch, for dusting

To make the red bean paste, place the adzuki beans in a large pot and add water until the beans are completely submerged. Cover the pot with a lid and bring to a boil. Turn the heat down to medium and cook for 1 hour to 1 hour and 30 minutes, or until the beans are easily mashed between your fingers. Drain the beans and place them in the bowl of a food processor. Add the brown sugar and oil, and process until smooth. Return the bean puree to the pot and cook on medium heat for 5 to 10 minutes, or until the mixture has thickened. It should be thick enough to hold a line when a utensil is drawn across the base of the pot. Remove from the heat and transfer the red bean paste to a shallow dish. Cover with cling wrap and chill for 2 hours to firm up, then roll into ten equal portions.

Line a baking tray with baking paper.

Prepare the mochi dough as per the Mochi Base recipe (page 24), using milk instead of water. Cool for 30 minutes or until completely cooled. To shape the mochi, wear food-safe gloves greased with vegetable oil. This prevents the mochi from sticking to your hands while keeping the mochi tacky enough to enclose the filling. Divide the mochi into ten equal balls and place them on the prepared tray. Flatten each ball between your palms.

To assemble the mochi, trim the strawberries and wrap each strawberry in a portion of cooled red bean paste. Then place a red bean–wrapped strawberry, pointy end down, in the center of a portion of mochi and bring the edges of the mochi together to enclose the strawberry, pinching the edges to seal. Dust with cornstarch and repeat until all the mochi balls have been used.

These are best the day they're made as mochi firms up over time. Store any remaining mochi in an airtight container at room temperature for up to 2 days.

tiramisu mochi

A fusion between Asia and Italy?! A strange but delicious concept, these mochi are inspired by the flavors of tiramisu. Chewy coffee-flavored mochi instead of coffee-soaked ladyfingers are filled with a vanilla mascarpone cream and sweet coffee jam. Completely unlike any traditional mochi, this is a new dessert in itself.

makes 10 mochi

coffee jam

1 tbsp (13 g) granulated sugar

1 tsp instant coffee powder

¼ cup (60 ml) heavy cream

mascarpone cream

½ cup (120 ml) heavy cream

¼ cup + 2 tbsp (75 g) granulated sugar

8 oz (225 g) mascarpone cheese

1 tsp rum, optional

mochi base

1 batch Mochi Base (page 24)

1 cup (240 ml) brewed coffee

assembly

1 cup (90 g) cocoa powder, for rolling

To make the coffee jam, combine the sugar, coffee powder and cream in a small saucepan over low heat. Heat over high heat for 5 minutes, or until a thick glossy jam forms. Remove from the heat and cool for 30 minutes, or until completely cooled. Transfer to a piping bag and set aside.

To make the mascarpone cream, line a baking tray with baking paper. In the bowl of a stand mixer fitted with a whisk attachment, combine the cream and sugar. Whisk on medium-high speed for 4 minutes, or until medium-stiff peaks form. Add the mascarpone cheese and rum, if using, and whisk for another 1 minute, or until combined and stiff peaks have formed. Transfer the cream to a piping bag fitted with a large round tip. Pipe ten round mounds of cream onto the prepared tray. Cut the tip off the coffee jam piping bag and insert it into the center of each mound. Squeeze the piping bag to fill the mounds with coffee jam. Place in the freezer to set for 1 hour, or until firm.

To make the mochi base, line another baking tray with baking paper. Prepare the mochi dough as per the Mochi Base recipe (page 24), using coffee instead of water. Cool for 30 minutes or until completely cooled. To shape the mochi, wear food-safe gloves greased with vegetable oil. This prevents the mochi from sticking to your hands while keeping the mochi tacky enough to enclose the filling. Divide the mochi into ten equal balls and place them on the prepared tray. Flatten each ball in between your palms.

To assemble, place the cocoa powder in a shallow bowl. Place a frozen mound of cream in the center of a mochi portion and bring the edges of the mochi together to enclose the filling. Pinch to seal, roll in cocoa powder and repeat until all the mochi balls have been used. Let sit for 15 minutes to allow the cream to defrost before enjoying.

These are best the day they're made as mochi firms up over time. Reserve them in the fridge until they're ready to be served and store any remaining mochi in an airtight container in the fridge for up to 2 days.

mochi ice cream

The perfect contrast in textures, this treat is made up of creamy ice cream in a thin, soft mochi skin. First popularized in Japan, and now the most popular kind of mochi all over the world, mochi ice cream can be found in most supermarkets! While it may be widely available, when you make homemade mochi ice cream, you have your choice of flavors. Whether you use your favorite store-bought ice cream or an easy version made from scratch, it's up to you; the options are endless. Choose between matcha, ube and strawberry, or divide your batter into thirds and do all three!

makes 10 mochi

special equipment

Hemisphere mold

easy ice cream

2 cups (480 ml) heavy cream

¾ cup (180 ml) condensed milk

2 tsp (4 g) matcha powder, optional

¼ tsp ube extract, optional

2 tbsp (12 g) freeze-dried strawberry powder, optional

Or 10 scoops of store-bought ice cream

mochi base variation

1 cup (130 g) glutinous rice flour

½ cup (100 g) granulated sugar

¼ cup (30 g) cornstarch

1 cup (240 ml) whole milk

1 tbsp (15 ml) vegetable oil

To make the easy ice cream, add the cream to the bowl of a stand mixer and whisk on medium-high speed for 5 minutes, or until it forms stiff peaks. Add the condensed milk and your desired flavoring, if using, and whisk until just combined. Fill ten cavities of a hemisphere mold and level the tops with an offset spatula. Freeze overnight, or for a minimum of 6 hours. This ensures the ice cream stays frozen as you wrap it in the mochi.

If using store-bought ice cream, line a cupcake tray with ten paper cases. Scoop ten balls of ice cream and place them in the lined tray. Freeze overnight or for a minimum of 4 hours.

To make the mochi base variation, follow the method for the Mochi Base (page 24), using the variation ingredient ratios and milk instead of water. Cool for 30 minutes or until completely cooled. This mochi base variation requires more sugar as it prevents the mochi from firming up in the freezer.

To assemble the mochi ice cream, line a baking tray with baking paper and wear food-safe gloves greased with vegetable oil. This prevents the mochi from sticking to your hands while keeping the mochi tacky enough to enclose the filling. Divide the mochi into ten equal balls and place them on a tray lined with baking paper. Unmold the ice cream from the silicone molds or remove the ice cream scoops from the cupcake cases. Flatten each mochi ball into a thin, large round between your palms. Place a frozen ice cream hemisphere in the center, round side down, and stretch the edges of the mochi over the ice cream to enclose. Pinch to seal, roll in cornstarch and repeat. Freeze for a minimum of 1 hour before enjoying.

These are best the day they're made as mochi firms up over time. Reserve them in the freezer until they're ready to be served and allow them to sit at room temperature for 15 minutes before consuming to allow the mochi to soften up. Store any remaining mochi in an airtight container in the freezer for up to 3 days.

espresso brown butter mochi brownies

With an increasing number of hybrid Franken-desserts, this brownie and mochi combination is one you can't miss. Similar to Hawaiian "butter mochi," a baked mochi slab made from glutinous rice flour and coconut milk, this version uses whole milk and espresso to create a rich and chocolatey mochi treat with a chewy, fudgy texture.

makes 1 (8-inch [20-cm]) square slab or 12 brownies

6 tbsp (90 g) unsalted butter, cubed

2 tsp (4 g) instant coffee powder

1 cup (130 g) glutinous rice flour

¾ cup (150 g) granulated sugar

½ cup (40 g) cocoa powder

1½ tsp (7 g) baking powder

¼ tsp salt

1½ cups (360 ml) whole milk

2 large eggs

3.5 oz (100 g) dark chocolate, 45% cocoa, roughly chopped

Flakey salt, optional

To make the mochi brownies, preheat the oven to 350°F (180°C) and line an 8 x 8-inch (20 x 20-cm) square tin with baking paper. In a small saucepan over medium heat, heat the butter for 3 minutes, or until melted. Continue to heat the butter, swirling the pan occasionally, for 3 to 5 minutes, until browned and fragrant. You will notice toasted milk solids on the bottom of the pan. Remove from the heat and add the coffee powder, stir until melted, and set aside. Cool for 15 minutes, or until at room temperature.

In a large mixing bowl, whisk the glutinous rice flour, sugar, cocoa powder, baking powder and salt until combined. Add the milk, cooled coffee brown butter and eggs, and whisk until smooth. Fold in the roughly chopped chocolate and pour the batter into the lined baking tin. Bake for 40 to 45 minutes, or until an inserted toothpick emerges slightly gooey. Remove from the oven and cool completely.

Once cooled, sprinkle with flakey salt, if using, and use a sharp, oiled knife to cut the slab into twelve squares. Serve at room temperature for a chewy brownie or warmed for a stretchy, gooey chocolate experience. Store in an airtight container at room temperature for up to 3 days.

molten salted egg sesame balls

These are a twist on the classic sesame balls, called zhīmáqíu (芝麻球) in Mandarin or jian dui (煎鎚) in Cantonese. Rather than a traditional sweetened red bean paste filling, they are filled with a sweet and salty duck egg custard. Salted duck eggs are a delicacy in East and Southeast Asian cuisine, made by soaking fresh duck eggs in salty brine (they can also be sold pre-cooked and separated). This preserves the eggs, giving them a unique salty flavor. While salted eggs are usually served as a congee condiment or cooked in savory dishes, they work great in desserts too because of that sweet-salty flavor combination.

makes 12 sesame balls

salted egg yolk filling

3 salted duck egg yolks, cooked (see Note)

3 tbsp (45 g) unsalted butter, room temperature

⅓ cup (35 g) powdered sugar

2 tbsp (24 g) custard powder

2 tbsp (13 g) milk powder

dough

1 cup (130 g) glutinous rice flour

⅓ cup (65 g) granulated sugar

½ cup (120 ml) boiling water

1 tbsp (15 ml) vegetable oil

assembly

⅔ cup (95 g) white sesame seeds, for rolling

Water, for dipping

Vegetable oil, for frying

Note: *Salted duck eggs can be found raw or cooked at most Asian grocery stores. If cooked, scoop out the yolks, and if raw separate the egg yolks from the whites and steam them for 15 minutes.*

To make the salted egg yolk filling, use a fork to mash the salted duck egg yolks into a paste. In a large mixing bowl, combine the egg yolks, butter, powdered sugar, custard powder and milk powder, and mix until well combined. Cover with cling wrap and chill for 30 minutes, or until firm. Then, roll into twelve equal balls and set aside.

To make the dough, combine the glutinous rice flour and sugar in a large heatproof bowl, and whisk to combine. Add the boiling water and mix until a shaggy dough forms, then use your hands to knead it into a rough dough. Add the vegetable oil and continue to knead until smooth. The dough should have the texture of an earlobe. If it's too dry add a splash of water, and if it's too wet add a little more glutinous rice flour. Cover with cling wrap and rest for 30 minutes.

To assemble the sesame balls, prepare two small bowls. Fill one bowl with the sesame seeds and the other with cold water. Portion the dough into twelve equal balls. Flatten each ball of dough between your palms and place a ball of salted egg filling in the center. Tightly pinch the edges of the dough to seal the custard and roll between your palms for a smooth finish. Dip the ball into the water, then into the sesame seeds, rolling to coat the entire surface. Gently roll the ball between your palms to secure the sesame seeds and repeat with the remaining dough.

To fry the sesame balls, bring a heavy-bottomed pot of vegetable oil, or a deep fryer, to 300°F (150°C). Gently place half the sesame balls in the oil and cook for 5 minutes, or until they float to the surface. Increase the heat to 350°F (180°C) and fry for another 2 to 3 minutes until golden brown. Remove from the oil, drain on a wire rack or paper towel, and cool for 5 minutes before enjoying. Repeat with the other half of the sesame balls.

These are best enjoyed warm as the mochi is still crispy, and the filling is warm and lava-like. Store any remaining sesame balls in an airtight container in the fridge for up to 2 days, and heat in the oven or microwave before consuming.

nutty mochi

These nutty mochi are a variation on the traditional peanut-filled lo mai chi (糯米糍), but with nuttier flavor. Traditionally rolled in coconut and filled with a sweet peanut and coconut filling, this variation is filled with a fragrant, nutty combination of peanut and hazelnuts and rolled in peanut powder.

makes 10 mochi

mochi base

1 batch Mochi Base (page 24)

1 cup (240 ml) whole milk

nutty filling

½ cup (65 g) whole hazelnuts

½ cup (75 g) whole peanuts

⅓ cup (65 g) granulated sugar

assembly

1 cup (65 g) peanut or soybean powder, for rolling

Prepare the mochi base as per the Mochi Base recipe (page 24), using whole milk instead of water. Cool completely.

Preheat the oven to 340°F (170°C) and place the hazelnuts and peanuts on a baking tray. Bake the nuts for 25 minutes or until they're golden brown and roasted. Cool for 30 minutes, or until they're at room temperature, and rub with a clean tea towel to remove the skins.

To make the nutty filling, combine the roasted nuts and sugar in the bowl of a food processor and pulse until they form a coarse powder.

To assemble the mochi, wear food-safe gloves greased with vegetable oil. This prevents the mochi from sticking to your hands while keeping the mochi tacky enough to enclose the filling. Divide the mochi into ten equal balls and place them on a baking tray lined with baking paper. Flatten each ball between your palms and place a heaped tablespoon of filling in the center. Bring the edges of the mochi together to enclose the filling, then pinch to seal and roll in the peanut powder. Repeat until all the mochi has been used. If you can't find peanut powder in your local Asian market, feel free to use finely crushed peanuts or soybean powder.

These are best the day they're made as mochi firms up over time. Reserve them in the fridge until they're ready to be served and store any remaining mochi in an airtight container at room temperature for up to 2 days.

cookies and cream snow skin mooncakes

Mooncakes are a traditional Chinese treat enjoyed during the Mid-Autumn Festival. During this time of year, the moon is its fullest and brightest, and families come together to watch the moon and celebrate the mid-autumn harvest. There are so many different kinds of mooncakes, each originating from different provinces of China, but snow skin mooncakes are a newer variety! Encased in soft mochi-like skin, the fillings range from traditional bean and lotus seed pastes to custards and ice cream. This fun take on the mooncake is filled with a smooth and crunchy "cookies and cream" filling.

makes 5 large mooncakes

special equipment

1 (3.5-oz [100-g]) mooncake mold

snow skin

⅓ cup (43 g) glutinous rice flour

¼ cup (40 g) rice flour

2 tbsp + 2 tsp (20 g) cornstarch

1 tbsp + 1 tsp (20 g) granulated sugar

½ cup + 2 tbsp (150 ml) whole milk

1 tbsp + 1 tsp (20 g) vegetable oil

cookie filling

6 (60 g) chocolate sandwich cookies

9 oz (250 g) cream cheese, room temperature, cubed

½ cup (50 g) powdered sugar

1 tsp vanilla extract

assembly

Glutinous rice flour, for dusting

To make the snow skin, combine the glutinous rice flour, rice flour, cornstarch, sugar and milk in a heatproof bowl, and whisk to combine. Cover the bowl with cling wrap and place in a steamer for 20 minutes, or until the center is fully cooked and no longer milky. Remove from the heat and cool for 30 minutes or until cool enough to handle.

Once the snow skin has cooled, add the oil, and using gloved or oiled hands knead the cooled dough until smooth. Kneading the dough helps incorporate the oil while enhancing the snow skin's chewy texture. Cover with cling wrap and reserve in the fridge until assembly.

To make the cookie filling, place the cookies in a sandwich bag and roughly crush with a rolling pin. In the bowl of a stand mixer fitted with a paddle attachment, combine the cream cheese, powdered sugar and vanilla extract, and beat on medium-high speed for 4 minutes, or until smooth. Remove the bowl from the stand mixer and fold in the crushed cookies. Chill for 30 minutes, or until firm, and roll into five equal balls.

To assemble the mooncakes, line a baking tray with baking paper. Divide the snow skin dough into five equal balls. Lightly coat each ball in glutinous rice flour. Flatten a ball and roll it out with a rolling pin to form a circle of approximately 4.3 inches (11 cm). Place a ball of cookie filling in the center of the rolled-out snow skin and pull the sides of the snow skin in to enclose the filling. Smooth the surface of the dough by rolling it between your palms and place the ball seam side up on the prepared tray. Dust the mooncake mold to prevent the dough from sticking, and place the mold over the filled dough and press down firmly to shape it into a mooncake. Repeat with the remaining dough and filling. Once molded, place in an airtight container and chill for 1 to 2 hours before serving. This helps the mooncakes set into their shape.

These are best the day they're made as glutinous rice flour firms up over time. Reserve them in the fridge until they're ready to be served and store any remaining mooncakes in an airtight container in the fridge for up to 2 days.

light, fluffy cakes

My absolute favorite kind of cake or dessert is one dressed in fresh cream. Who needs greasy, sweet buttercreams when you can have cakes frosted in a light, freshly whipped cream?

Not only does fresh whipped cream add another layer of texture to a cake, but it also has the ability to neutralize sweetness and bring balance. This is the secret to most Asian cakes and desserts. A little cream can bring back a rich ganache or add sweetness to a plain sponge. Its ability to enhance cakes is endless and so are its applications!

And if there is a kind of cake that is perfect for whipped cream, it's a light sponge cake. Thanks to its spongy, airy texture, it is able to take on the flavors of creams, fillings and syrups. That's why sponge cakes are always so much better the second day! All the cakes in this chapter follow the same principle, with each filling, cream and flavoring helping to lift the other elements and come together to form the perfect cake.

The recipes in this chapter cover trending cakes on social media like cute Cherry Lunch Box Cakes (page 63) and Chiffon Boba Lava Cake (page 60) as well as the quintessential cake found in all Asian bakeries: Japanese Strawberry Shortcake (page 48). There is no shortage of potential celebration cakes or little treats for afternoon tea, all of course with a touch of Asian inspiration.

japanese strawberry shortcake

If I could pick a single recipe for you to make from this book, it would be this one. This Japanese Strawberry Shortcake is a classic, and I would even call this the quintessential Asian cake. Growing up, Asian-style sponge cakes were always my favorite kind of dessert. The combination of cloud-like sponge cake and whipped cream is so light, I could eat it forever. I have made it a mission since the very beginning of my baking journey to master this cake and am proud to say this is the closest I'll ever get. I've baked hundreds of sponge cakes so you could all enjoy the very best strawberry shortcake!

makes 1 (8-inch [20-cm]) cake

sponge cake

Cotton-Soft Sponge Cake Base, 8-inch (20-cm) (page 19)

simple syrup

⅓ cup (65 g) granulated sugar

⅓ cup (80 ml) water

glaze

¼ cup (80 g) apricot jam

1 tbsp (15 ml) water

whipped cream

2½ cups (600 ml) heavy cream

½ cup (100 g) granulated sugar

1 tsp vanilla extract

assembly

13 oz (370 g) strawberries, divided

Prepare the sponge cake as per the Cotton-Soft Sponge Cake Base recipe for an 8-inch (20-cm) cake (page 19). Place in the fridge and chill for 1 to 2 hours or until completely cooled.

To make the simple syrup, combine the sugar and water in a small saucepan over low heat, stirring occasionally, for 3 to 4 minutes, until the sugar has completely dissolved. Remove from the heat and cool for 30 minutes or until completely cooled.

To make the glaze, combine the jam and water in a small saucepan over low heat for 3 to 4 minutes until melted together. Pour through a fine-meshed sieve and set aside.

To make the whipped cream, combine the cream, sugar and vanilla in the bowl of a stand mixer fitted with a whisk attachment, and whisk on medium-high speed for 5 minutes until the mixture forms medium-stiff peaks. Cover with cling wrap and reserve in the fridge until use.

Prepare the cake for assembly by trimming the top and slicing the cake into three equal layers with a serrated knife. Select six perfect strawberries for decoration and thinly slice the remaining strawberries. Place a layer of cake on a cake board, and place both on a turntable. Using a pastry brush, brush the cake layer with simple syrup. Then spread a thin layer of whipped cream over the cake and top with a layer of sliced strawberries and another thin layer of cream. Place the next cake layer on top and repeat before topping with the final layer of sponge cake. Using a large palette knife, spread two-thirds of the remaining whipped cream over the cake, spinning the turntable as you go to create a smooth finish.

Transfer the remaining whipped cream to a piping bag fitted with a large French star tip and pipe a border around the top edge of the cake. Slice the remaining six strawberries in half and arrange them on top of the cake. Lightly brush the strawberries with the glaze and chill the cake for 1 to 2 hours to set.

This cake is best enjoyed chilled; reserve the cake in the fridge until it is ready to be served. The cake can be stored in an airtight container in the fridge for up to 3 days.

chocolate cherry pocky cake

Pocky (ポッキー) or Peppero (빼빼로), chocolate-covered pretzels, are one of the most popular snacks in Japan and South Korea. These simple yet delicious snacks are an iconic Asian treat, and are widely available in grocery stores around the world. This cake takes the classic chocolate–cherry flavor combination and enhances it with a delicious and crunchy border of chocolate pretzels to create a stunning cake that requires little to no decorating skill!

makes 1 (6-inch [15-cm]) cake

chocolate whipped ganache

2 cups (480 ml) heavy cream, divided

5.6 oz (160 g) semi-sweet chocolate, 45% cocoa, finely chopped

chocolate sponge cake

Cotton-Soft Sponge Cake Base, 6-inch (15-cm), Chocolate Sponge Cake variation (page 19)

simple syrup

⅓ cup (65 g) granulated sugar

⅓ cup (80 ml) water

assembly

2 cups (280 g) cherries, divided

5.35 oz (150 g) chocolate Pocky

To make the chocolate whipped ganache, heat 1 cup (240 ml) of cream in a small saucepan over medium heat for 4 minutes, or until steaming. Place the chocolate in a large heatproof bowl and pour the steaming cream over it. Cover with a plate and let sit for 5 to 10 minutes, until the chocolate has completely melted. Stir until smooth, then add the remaining cream and stir until well combined. Cover with cling wrap and chill overnight, or for a minimum of 4 hours.

Prepare the sponge as per the 6-inch (15-cm) Cotton-Soft Sponge Cake Base recipe using the Chocolate Sponge Cake variation (page 19).

To make the simple syrup, combine the sugar and water in a small saucepan over low heat, stirring occasionally, for 3 to 4 minutes, until the sugar has completely dissolved. Remove from the heat and cool for 30 minutes or until completely cooled.

To finish the whipped ganache, pour the chilled chocolate ganache into the bowl of a stand mixer fitted with a whisk attachment and whisk on medium-high speed for 4 minutes, until stiff peaks form. *Keep a close eye on the ganache while whipping, as it splits easily. Stop mixing as soon as stiff peaks form.* Cover with cling wrap and reserve in the fridge until ready to use.

Prepare the cake for assembly by trimming the top and slicing the cake into three equal layers with a serrated knife. Pit and halve 1 cup (140 g) of the cherries. Place a layer of cake on a cake board, and place both on a turntable. Using a pastry brush, brush the cake layer with simple syrup. Then spread a thin layer of whipped ganache over the cake, top with a layer of cherries, cut side down, and add another thin layer of ganache. Place the next cake layer on top and repeat before topping with the final layer of sponge cake. Using a palette knife, spread the remaining whipped ganache over the cake, spinning the turntable as you go to create a smooth finish.

To decorate, arrange the Pocky around the top edge of the cake and fill the center with the remaining cherries. Chill the cake for 1 to 2 hours to set.

This cake is best enjoyed chilled; reserve the cake in the fridge until ready to be served. The cake can be stored in an airtight container in the fridge for up to 3 days. Keep in mind that the Pocky will get soggier the longer the cake is kept.

matcha red bean roll cake

Matcha and red bean are both earthy flavors. But together, and with a touch of sugar, they make a delicious combination found across East Asia, most commonly in traditional Japanese sweets like mochi. This is a classic example of a Western dessert modified for the Asian palette: a semi-sweet soft matcha cake that encapsulates the flavors of Japan!

makes 1 roll cake

red bean paste

¼ cup (50 g) adzuki (red) beans

Water, to cover the beans

¼ cup (45 g) brown sugar, unpacked

2 tsp (10 ml) vegetable oil

matcha roll cake

Roll Cake Base, Matcha Roll Cake variation (page 16)

matcha cream

¾ cup (180 ml) heavy cream

2 tbsp (25 g) granulated sugar

1 tbsp (6 g) matcha powder

To make the red bean paste, place the adzuki beans in a large pot and add water until the beans are completely submerged. Cover the pot with a lid and bring to a boil. Turn the heat down to medium and cook for 1 hour to 1 hour and 30 minutes, or until the beans are easily mashed between your fingers. Drain the beans and return them to the pot. Add the brown sugar and cook over medium heat for 5 minutes, or until the sugar has melted and the mixture has thickened. It should be thick enough to hold a line when a utensil is drawn across the base of the pot. Stir in the oil, remove from the heat and chill for 1 hour or until completely cooled.

Prepare the cake as per the Roll Cake Base recipe using the Matcha Roll Cake variation (page 16).

To make the matcha cream, combine the cream and sugar in the bowl of a stand mixer fitted with a whisk attachment. Sieve in the matcha powder and whisk the cream on medium-high speed for 5 minutes, or until stiff peaks form. Cover with cling wrap and reserve in the fridge until ready to use.

To assemble the roll cake, carefully unravel the cooled roll cake. Spread a layer of red bean paste over the inside of the cake roll, followed by a layer of matcha cream. Spread a thicker layer of cream closer to the center of the roll and a thinner layer closer to the unraveled edge. This prevents excess cream from escaping once rolled. Carefully roll the cake up, following the curl of the cake, and wrap tightly in cling wrap. Chill overnight, or for a minimum of 3 hours to set before trimming the ends and serving.

This cake is best enjoyed chilled; reserve the cake in the fridge until ready to be served. The cake can be stored in an airtight container in the fridge for up to 3 days.

thai tea mille crêpe

Crêpe cake or *gâteau mille crêpes*, meaning "a thousand crêpes cake," is a classic French pastry. While this cake might not be made of a thousand crêpes, the 25 or so crêpe layers create a stunning dessert. This may be one of the more time-consuming cakes in this chapter, but the end result won't disappoint and the feeling of sinking your fork through the layers of delicate crêpes and cream is so worth it! The addition of a spiced Thai milk tea cream and vibrant, creamy sauce creates a delicious and uniquely spiced dessert.

makes 1 large crêpe cake

thai tea cream

3½ cups (840 ml) heavy cream

½ cup (40 g) Thai tea mix

1 cup (200 g) granulated sugar

crêpe batter

2 cups (480 ml) whole milk

¾ cup + 2 tbsp (110 g) all-purpose flour

½ cup (60 g) cornstarch

¼ cup (50 g) granulated sugar

6 large eggs

2 tbsp (30 g) unsalted butter, melted

Vegetable oil, for greasing

thai tea sauce

¼ cup (20 g) Thai tea mix

½ cup (120 ml) condensed milk

½ cup (120 ml) whole milk

2 tbsp (30 g) unsalted butter

To make the Thai tea cream, combine the cream and Thai tea mix in a small saucepan over medium heat. Bring to a boil and remove from the heat. Cover and chill overnight, or for a minimum of 6 hours to allow the cream to infuse.

Once the cream has chilled, remove it from the fridge and pour through a fine-meshed sieve or cheesecloth into the bowl of a stand mixer fitted with a whisk attachment. Add the sugar and whisk the cream on medium-high speed for 5 minutes, or until stiff peaks form. Cover with cling wrap and reserve in the fridge until ready to use.

To make the crêpes, combine the milk, flour, cornstarch, sugar, eggs and butter in a blender and blitz for 10 seconds, or until smooth. Pour the batter through a fine-meshed sieve into a large bowl and set it aside.

To cook the crêpes, soak a paper towel with vegetable oil and lightly grease a medium-sized (9.5-inch [24-cm]) frypan. Heat the greased pan over medium-low heat until it's hot. Add ¼ cup (60 ml) of batter, or enough to coat the surface of the pan, and swirl the pan to create an even layer. Gently heat the crêpe for 2 to 3 minutes, until the surface becomes matte, then flip and cook the opposite side for 10 seconds. Remove it from the pan and cool on a baking tray. Repeat with the remaining batter and allow the crêpes to come to room temperature.

To assemble the cake, place a cake board or plate on a turntable. Make sure you build the cake on a serving surface as it will be difficult to move the cake once assembled. Lay one crêpe on the board or plate and spread a thin layer of Thai tea cream over it. Top with another crêpe. Repeat the process until all the crêpes have been used. Chill overnight, or for a minimum of 3 hours to set.

To make the Thai tea sauce, combine the Thai tea mix, condensed milk, whole milk and butter in a small saucepan over medium heat and bring to a boil. Reduce the heat to medium-high and cook for 4 to 5 minutes until thickened. Remove from the heat and pour through a fine-meshed sieve or cheesecloth into a pouring jug. Cool for 1 hour, or until completely cooled.

Once the cake has set, slice and serve with a drizzle of Thai tea sauce. This cake is best enjoyed chilled and can be stored in an airtight container in the fridge for up to 3 days.

matcha tiramisu

This matcha-flavored dessert is another one of my takes on the Italian classic tiramisu. Tiramisu is usually made with raw egg yolks, but heating them over a hot water bath helps to pasteurize them and ensure they are safe for consumption. Not only that, but the egg yolks also add an extra creaminess to the mascarpone cream for a rich flavor, so don't leave them out! In this case, matcha works great in place of espresso, as its grassy, slightly bitter flavor complements the sweet mascarpone cream . . . I guess you could call it a tea-ramisu!

makes 3 (2-cup [500-ml]) or 1 (6-cup [1.5-L]) servings

ladyfingers

3 large eggs, whites and yolks separated

½ cup (100 g) granulated sugar

¾ cup (90 g) all-purpose flour

¼ cup (25 g) powdered sugar, for dusting

matcha syrup

1½ tbsp (9 g) matcha powder, or to taste

¼ cup (50 g) granulated sugar

1 cup (240 ml) boiling water

mascarpone cream

3 large egg yolks

⅓ cup (65 g) granulated sugar

1 tbsp (15 ml) rum, optional

1 tsp vanilla extract

8 oz (225 g) mascarpone cheese

1 cup (240 ml) heavy cream

assembly

Matcha powder, for dusting

To make the tiramisu, prepare one 8 x 8-inch (20 x 20–cm) dish or three 3.5 x 3.5–inch (9 x 9–cm) dishes (these serving dishes are both suggestions!).

To make the ladyfingers, preheat the oven to 340°F (170°C) and line a large baking tray with baking paper. In the bowl of a stand mixer fitted with a whisk attachment, add the egg whites. Whisk on medium-high speed for 1 to 2 minutes, until the egg whites are foamy, then add the granulated sugar and continue beating for 4 minutes, or until the meringue forms stiff peaks. Add the egg yolks and whisk until combined. Remove the bowl from the stand mixer and sieve in the flour, folding it in until just combined. Transfer the batter to a piping bag fitted with a medium-sized piping tip and pipe 3.5-inch (9-cm) lines of batter on the lined baking tray. Place the powdered sugar in a fine-meshed sieve and generously dust the piped batter, then bake for 15 minutes or until lightly golden brown. Cool for 30 minutes, or until completely cooled.

To make the matcha syrup, sieve the matcha powder into a small bowl. Add the sugar and boiling water, and whisk until the sugar has dissolved. Set aside to cool for 30 minutes, or until completely cooled.

To make the mascarpone cream, bring a small saucepan of water to a simmer. In a heatproof bowl slightly larger than the saucepan, combine the egg yolks and sugar. Place the bowl over the saucepan and heat gently, whisking constantly, for 5 minutes, or until the sugar has dissolved and the egg yolks have doubled in volume. Remove from the heat and add the rum, if using, vanilla extract and mascarpone cheese. Whisk until smooth and set aside. In the bowl of a stand mixer fitted with a whisk attachment, add the cream and whisk on medium-high speed for 5 minutes, or until it forms stiff peaks. Then, fold the whipped cream into the mascarpone mixture until just combined.

To assemble, submerge a ladyfinger in the matcha syrup and quickly place it in the bottom of your prepared dish. Continue until the bottom of your dish is covered. Top with a layer of cream, another layer of soaked ladyfingers and a final layer of cream. Smooth the top layer with an offset spatula and chill overnight, or for a minimum of 4 hours, until set.

Once the tiramisu has set, dust with matcha powder and enjoy. The cake can be covered in cling wrap and stored in the fridge for up to 3 days.

ube roll cake

This ube roll is a twist on a Filipino cake called a pianono, a rolled cake traditionally filled with softened margarine and sugar. These days pianono are made with all kinds of fillings, from jams to fresh fruits . . . and in this case, ube cream. Ube, or purple yam, is a sweet root vegetable with a nutty and vanilla-like flavor that is delicious in desserts and increasing in popularity all over the world. It's not just known for its unique and delicious flavor; its vibrant purple color is catching everyone's attention, as will this cake!

makes 1 roll cake

ube roll cake

Roll Cake Base, Ube Roll Cake variation (page 16)

ube cream

¾ cup (180 ml) heavy cream

2 tbsp (25 g) granulated sugar

1 tsp ube extract

Prepare the cake as per the Roll Cake Base recipe using the Ube Roll Cake variation (page 16).

To make the ube cream, combine the cream, sugar and ube extract in the bowl of a stand mixer fitted with a whisk attachment, and whisk on medium-high speed for 5 minutes or until the mixture forms stiff peaks. Cover with cling wrap and reserve in the fridge until ready to use.

To assemble the roll cake, carefully unravel the cooled roll cake. Spread a layer of ube cream over the inside of the cake roll. Make sure to spread a thicker layer of cream closer to the center of the roll and a thinner layer closer to the unraveled edge. This prevents excess cream from escaping once rolled. Carefully roll the cake up, following the curl of the cake, and wrap tightly in cling wrap. Chill overnight, or for a minimum of 3 hours to set before trimming the ends and serving.

This cake is best enjoyed chilled; reserve the cake in the fridge until ready to be served. The cake can be stored in an airtight container in the fridge for up to 3 days.

chiffon boba lava cake

Brown sugar boba is all the rage! Originating in Taiwan, this sweet milky drink has been showing up in all kinds of desserts, from ice cream to cake. This cake was inspired by the trending Taiwanese boba cake, a small cake with a plastic collar that when lifted oozes a lava-like boba-flavored cream. This larger cake is made with a black tea chiffon base for a cloud-like sponge and when sliced reveals a puddle of delicious milk tea custard and boba for a fun cake that is bound to impress. I've included a recipe for homemade boba, which is soft and chewy, but quite labor-intensive. If you're short on time, store-bought pearls work just as well!

makes 1 (8-inch [20-cm]) chiffon cake

tea-infused milk

1 cup (240 ml) whole milk

2 tbsp (6 g) black tea

milk tea custard lava

1 batch Pastry Cream (page 20), prepared with tea-infused milk

¾ cup (180 ml) heavy cream

black tea chiffon cake

2 tbsp (6 g) black tea

½ cup (120 ml) water, boiling

6 large egg yolks

⅔ cup (130 g) superfine sugar, divided

⅓ cup + 1 tbsp (95 ml) vegetable oil

1¼ cups (150 g) cake flour

2 tsp (9 g) baking powder

6 large egg whites

To make the tea-infused milk, heat the milk and black tea in a small saucepan over medium heat for 3 minutes, until steaming. Remove from the heat and set aside to infuse for 30 minutes. Filter the tea leaves out by pouring the cream through a fine-meshed sieve or cheesecloth.

To make the milk tea custard lava, follow the Pastry Cream recipe (page 20), using the tea-infused milk instead of the plain whole milk.

Once cooled, place the pastry cream and heavy cream in the bowl of a stand mixer fitted with a whisk attachment. Whisk on medium speed for 3 minutes or until well combined and slightly thickened. Cover with cling wrap and reserve in the fridge until the cake is ready to assemble.

To make the black tea chiffon cake, preheat the oven to 340°F (170°C) and prepare an ungreased 8-inch (20-cm) chiffon cake tin with a removable base. It's important to use an ungreased cake tin as the cake uses the ungreased sides of the tin to rise. Combine the black tea and boiling water, set aside to cool, and infuse for 5 minutes. Do not strain. Meanwhile, in a medium-sized bowl, whisk the egg yolks and 3 tablespoons (40 g) of superfine sugar. Add the cooled black tea and oil, and whisk to combine. Sieve in the cake flour and baking powder, and whisk until just combined, then set aside.

In the bowl of a stand mixer fitted with a whisk attachment, add the egg whites and whisk on medium speed for 2 minutes or until foamy. Add ⅓ cup + 2 tablespoons (90 g) of superfine sugar and continue to whisk for 5 minutes until it forms stiff peaks. Add one-third of this meringue to the egg yolk mixture and whisk until well combined. Transfer the lightened egg yolk mixture to the remaining meringue and fold gently until just combined. Pour the batter into the cake tin and bake for 45 minutes, or until an inserted skewer emerges clean. Remove from the oven, invert the tin on a wire rack and cool completely. Once cooled, run a thin knife around the sides and base of the cake to unmold.

(continued)

chiffon boba lava cake *(continued)*

homemade brown sugar boba

¾ cup (90 g) tapioca starch

3 tbsp (35 g) brown sugar, unpacked

¼ cup (60 ml) water, boiling

Brown food coloring, optional

Tapioca starch for dusting

brown sugar syrup

¼ cup (45g) brown sugar, unpacked

To make the homemade boba, combine the tapioca starch, brown sugar, water and brown food coloring, if using, in a medium-sized heatproof bowl. Mix until a shaggy dough forms, then transfer the dough onto a bench lightly floured with tapioca starch and knead until smooth. Divide the dough into three equal portions and roll each portion into a log 10 mm wide. Working with one log at a time, cut off 10-mm pieces and roll them into balls before dusting them with tapioca starch. This prevents them from sticking to each other. While you are working on one log, keep the other logs covered with cling wrap to prevent them from drying out.

Bring a large pot of water to a boil over high heat and add the boba, stirring to prevent them from sticking to the bottom of the pot. Once the boba float to the surface, cover the pot, reduce the heat to medium and cook for 20 minutes, or until the boba are almost translucent. Turn off the heat and let them sit for 20 minutes before draining. Prepare the brown sugar syrup immediately after draining.

To make the brown sugar syrup, combine the cooked boba and brown sugar in a small saucepan over medium-high heat. Cook, stirring occasionally, for 10 minutes or until the sugar has thickened into a thick syrup. Remove from the heat and cool for 1 hour, or until room temperature.

To serve, invert the cake on a serving platter. Fill the center and cover the top with milk tea custard, allowing some to drip down the sides, then top with the brown sugar boba and consume immediately.

Boba will firm up if chilled, so if you're not consuming the whole cake, reserve some boba to be reheated when consuming next. Simply heat the boba up with a splash of water in a small saucepan or the microwave and serve with the remaining cake. The cake can be stored in an airtight container in the fridge for up to 3 days.

If you don't have time to make boba, feel free to substitute it with ½ cup (32 g) of store-bought instant boba, which is readily available at Asian markets. Simply follow the instructions on the package for a quick fix!

cherry lunch box cakes

Originating in the aesthetic cafés of South Korea, these minimalistic cakes served in paper boxes rose in popularity during the pandemic as cakes "on-the-go" or "for one." Without large gatherings, big celebratory cakes weren't really needed and small, cutely decorated cakes were the perfect gift no matter the occasion. These brightly colored sponge cakes are filled with fruity cherry jam and topped with a tangy cream cheese frosting. Change up the design and colors of these cakes to create the perfect gifts for your friends and family!

makes 3 (4-inch [10-cm]) cakes

sponge cake

Roll Cake Base, unrolled
(page 16)

cherry jam

5 oz (142 g) pitted cherries, roughly chopped

¼ cup (50 g) granulated sugar

1 tsp lemon juice

simple syrup

⅓ cup (65 g) granulated sugar

⅓ cup (80 ml) water

whipped cheese cream

12 oz (340 g) cream cheese

¼ cup (50 g) granulated sugar

1 cup (240 ml) heavy cream

Red, blue, green and pink food coloring

Prepare the sponge cake as per the Roll Cake Base recipe (page 16). Once the cake has baked, remove it from the baking pan. Do not roll it. Set it aside to cool for 1 hour, or until completely cooled. Once completely cooled, use a 4-inch (10-cm) round cutter to cut out six circles. If necessary, two half circles can be combined to create one whole circle.

Meanwhile, prepare the cherry jam. In a small saucepan over medium heat, combine the cherries, sugar and lemon juice, and cook for 5 minutes, stirring occasionally, until the cherries have broken down and thickened. Remove from the heat and cool completely.

To make the simple syrup, combine the sugar and water in a small saucepan over low heat, stirring occasionally, for 3 to 4 minutes, until the sugar has completely dissolved. Remove from the heat and cool for 30 minutes, or until completely cooled.

To make the whipped cheese cream, combine the cream cheese and sugar in the bowl of a stand mixer fitted with a whisk attachment and whisk on medium speed for 4 minutes, or until smooth and lightened. Add the cream and continue to whisk for 2 to 3 minutes, until the cream forms stiff peaks. Cover with cling wrap and reserve in the fridge until the cakes are ready to be assembled.

To assemble the cakes, place a small sheet of baking paper topped with a round of cake on a turntable. Using a pastry brush, brush the cake layer with simple syrup, then spread a thin layer of whipped cheese cream over the cake. Top with a layer of cherry jam and another round of cake. Clean up the edges and chill for 1 hour, or until set.

Divide the remaining cream into five bowls and color them red, blue, green and pink with a few drops of food coloring, leaving one white. Reserve in the fridge until ready to use.

(continued)

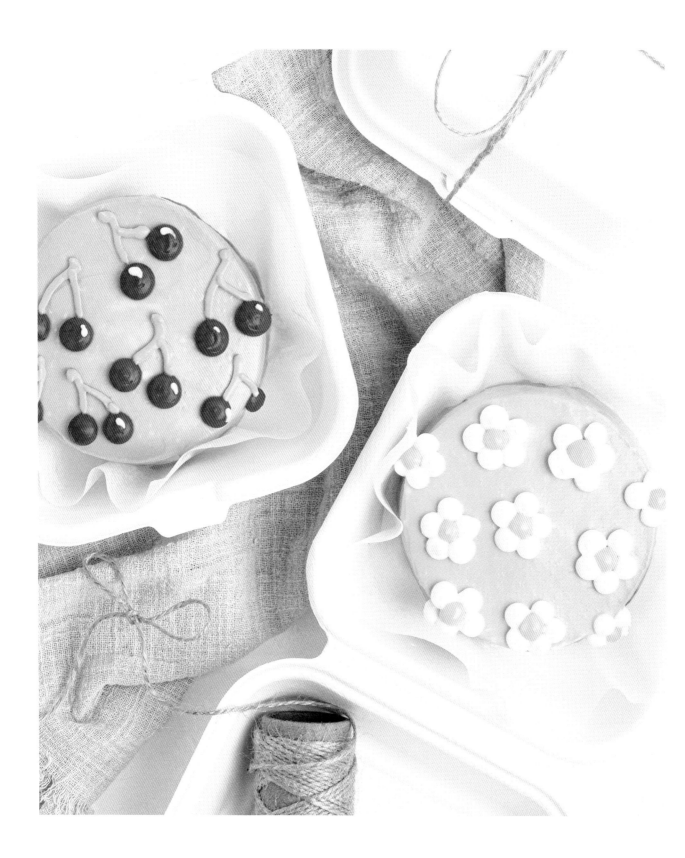

cherry lunch box cakes *(continued)*

Once the cakes have set, place them on the turntable and use a spatula to spread an even layer of cream in your desired color, spinning the turntable as you go to create a smooth finish. Transfer the remaining cream into piping bags fitted with small round tips and pipe your desired design over the cake. Use your imagination, or use my cakes for inspiration!

These cakes are best enjoyed chilled; reserve the cakes in the fridge until ready to be served. The cakes can be stored in an airtight container in the fridge for up to 4 days.

vietnamese coffee tres leches

Tres leches is a popular Latin American cake literally named "three milks" after the mixture of whole milk, sweetened condensed milk and evaporated milk the cake is soaked in. This technique gives an otherwise plain sponge cake so much flavor and moisture! I wanted to infuse this cake with an intense coffee flavor and there is nothing like a good cup of Vietnamese coffee. Vietnamese coffee is a much darker roast, and when filtered through a *phin*, or Vietnamese coffee filter, creates an intense and bitter cup of coffee that is usually served with sweetened condensed milk. This cake is inspired by the genius of Latin America and the flavors of Vietnam for a coffee experience like no other!

makes 1 (9 x 13-inch [22 x 33-cm]) sheet cake

cake

5 large egg yolks

½ cup (100 g) granulated sugar, divided

1 tsp vanilla extract

⅓ cup (80 ml) whole milk

1 cup (120 g) all-purpose flour

1 tsp baking powder

¼ tsp baking soda

5 large egg whites

vietnamese coffee soak

12 oz (340 g) evaporated milk

9 oz (255 g) condensed milk

¼ cup (60 ml) Vietnamese coffee, or espresso

¼ cup (60 ml) whole milk

coffee whipped cream

2 cups (480 ml) heavy cream

2 tsp (4 g) instant coffee powder, or to taste

½ cup (100 g) granulated sugar

assembly

Instant coffee powder for dusting

Preheat the oven to 350°F (180°C) and line a 9 x 13-inch (22 x 33-cm) rectangular pan with baking paper. In a large bowl, combine the egg yolks and ¼ cup (50 g) sugar, and whisk until lightened in color and doubled in volume. Add the vanilla extract and milk, and whisk until smooth. Then sieve in the flour, baking powder and baking soda, and whisk until just combined.

In the bowl of a stand mixer fitted with a whisk attachment, add the egg whites and whisk on medium-high for 2 minutes, or until the egg whites are foamy. Add ¼ cup (50 g) of sugar and continue to whisk for 5 minutes, or until the meringue forms stiff peaks. Fold one-third of the meringue into the egg yolk mixture and whisk until smooth. Transfer the lightened egg yolk mixture to the remaining meringue and gently fold until the batter is just combined. Transfer the batter to the lined rectangular pan and bake for 20 minutes, or until an inserted skewer emerges clean. Cool for 1 hour, or until completely cooled.

Meanwhile, in a jug, make the coffee soak by whisking the evaporated milk, condensed milk, coffee and milk. Once the cake has cooled completely, invert to remove the baking paper from the base and carefully place the cake back into the tin. Prick the cake all over with a fork and pour the coffee soak over the cake. Cover with cling wrap and place in the fridge to soak overnight, or for a minimum of 4 hours.

Once the cake has soaked, prepare the coffee whipped cream. In the bowl of a stand mixer fitted with a whisk attachment, combine the cream, instant coffee powder and sugar, and whisk on medium-high speed for 4 minutes, or until it forms medium-stiff peaks. Feel free to modify the amount of coffee used to your taste. Spoon the cream over the chilled cake and spread evenly. Dust with the instant coffee powder, then slice into squares to enjoy!

This cake is best enjoyed chilled; reserve the cake in the fridge until it's ready to be served. The cake can be stored in an airtight container in the fridge for up to 3 days.

cheesy cakes and other bakes

Cakes are the most important kind of dessert because they are an icon of celebration. Whether you're at a birthday, baby shower or wedding, you can't go without a cake. It brings people together and creates delicious memories. The cake possibilities are endless, and that's why this chapter brings more cakes!

Moving away from fresh cream-based cakes, the cakes here range from simple unfrosted chiffon cakes and cupcakes to cheesecakes in all shapes and forms. So, whether you are looking for a cake to celebrate a special event or simply find a fun weekend baking project, this chapter will cover everything you need.

Of the cakes in this chapter, a large segment covers cheesecakes! When you think of a cheesecake, you probably picture a classic New York–style cheesecake with a crushed cookie base and creamy cheese layer. Honestly, me too. A flavorful and rich baked cheesecake is my weakness . . . but there is so much more to the world of cheesecakes. I've included my absolute favorites in this chapter.

Aside from cheesecakes, I'm bringing you a range of Asian classics like Paper-Wrapped Chiffon Cupcakes (page 86) and Pandan Chiffon Cake (page 74) as well as new adaptations like Molten Hojicha Dulce de Leche Lava Cakes (page 82) or Coconut, Lychee and Raspberry Lamingtons (page 78). If you're looking for a new baking project here, you won't go astray!

baked ube cheesecake

Ube is a root vegetable originating in the Philippines, known for its bright purple color and sweet vanilla-like flavor. The earthy and nutty vanilla flavor of ube works so well with tangy cream cheese and comes together to make a stunning cheesecake. This baked cheesecake uses ube extract and jam to form two tones of purple in one cheesecake. If you want to make your life easier, feel free to add all the ube extract and jam to the batter to create an equally beautiful single layer of cheesecake with a Filipino twist.

makes a taller 7-inch (18-cm) or shorter 8-inch (20-cm) cheesecake

crust

5 oz (140 g) graham crackers or digestive biscuits

¼ cup (60 g) unsalted butter, melted

cheesecake filling

17.6 oz (500 g) cream cheese, room temperature

⅔ cup (130 g) granulated sugar

½ cup (120 ml) plain Greek yogurt or sour cream, room temperature

⅔ cup (160 ml) heavy cream

⅓ cup (80 g) ube jam (ube halaya)

1 tbsp (8 g) cornstarch

1 tsp vanilla extract

2 large eggs

½ tsp ube extract

whipped cream

¾ cup (180 ml) heavy cream

2 tbsp (25 g) granulated sugar

½ tsp vanilla extract

Crushed graham crackers or digestive biscuits, to decorate, optional

To make the cheesecake, preheat the oven to 340°F (170°C). Line the base of a 7-inch (18-cm) or 8-inch (20-cm) springform pan with baking paper and wrap the bottom in aluminum foil. The foil creates a barrier against the water bath the cake will bake in, so ensure the base is wrapped tightly to prevent water from seeping into the cake.

To make the crust, place the crackers in the bowl of a food processor and blitz until a fine crumb forms. Add the butter and pulse until combined. Transfer the crumbs to the lined tin and press into the base with a smooth bottomed object.

To make the cheesecake filling, place the cream cheese and sugar in the bowl of a stand mixer fitted with a paddle attachment and beat on medium speed for 3 minutes, or until smooth. Add the yogurt, cream, ube jam, cornstarch and vanilla, and continue to beat for 2 minutes, or until well combined. Add the eggs one at a time, beating in between each addition until smooth.

Transfer three-quarters of the batter to a medium-sized bowl. Add the ube extract, mix until smooth and pour the mixture into the graham cracker crust. Place the tin in a 9 x 13-inch (22 x 33–cm) rectangular pan and fill the pan with 0.8 inches (2 cm) of boiling water. Bake for 15 minutes, then remove and pour the remaining light purple batter into the tin. Bake for another 40 minutes, then turn off the oven and leave the cheesecake in for 30 minutes. Remove from the oven and cool to room temperature. Cover and chill overnight, or for a minimum of 4 hours.

To make the whipped cream, combine the cream, sugar and vanilla in the bowl of a stand mixer fitted with a whisk attachment and whisk on medium-high speed for 5 minutes, or until the cream forms stiff peaks. Transfer to a piping bag fitted with a star tip and reserve in the fridge until assembly.

Once the cheesecake has chilled, unmold it from the tin and pipe swirls of whipped cream around the top edge of the cake. Top with graham cracker crumbs if using.

This cake is best enjoyed chilled; reserve the cake in the fridge until it's ready to be served. The cake can be stored in an airtight container in the fridge for up to 3 days.

baked matcha chocolate terrine

A traditional French dish made from meats and vegetables, the terrine gets its name from the mold in which it's baked, and is a rectangular, gelatinous loaf that is typically served cold and sliced. Sweeter terrines have been rising in popularity, particularly in Japan and South Korea, over the past couple of years. The result is what can only be described as a cake-fudge-brownie hybrid with a smooth and fudgy texture. This version combines matcha and chocolate for a rich yet perfectly sweet terrine that can be enjoyed fudgy when cold or gooey when warm.

makes 1 (9 x 5-inch [22 x 13-cm]) loaf

matcha layer

⅓ cup + 1 tbsp (95 g) heavy cream

3 tbsp (45 g) unsalted butter, room temperature

7 oz (200 g) white chocolate, finely chopped

2 tbsp (15 g) cornstarch

2 tbsp (12 g) matcha powder

2 large eggs

chocolate layer

½ cup (120 ml) heavy cream

¼ cup (60 g) unsalted butter, room temperature

7 oz (200 g) dark chocolate, 70% cocoa, finely chopped

2 tbsp (15 g) cornstarch

3 tbsp (38 g) granulated sugar

2 large eggs

assembly

Cocoa powder for dusting

Whipped cream, optional

Ice cream, optional

To make the terrine, preheat the oven to 285°F (140°C) and line the bottom and sides of a 9 x 5-inch (22 x 13-cm) loaf tin with baking paper.

To make the matcha layer, heat the cream and butter in a small saucepan over medium heat for 4 minutes, or until steaming. Place the chocolate in a large heatproof bowl and pour the cream over the chocolate. Cover the bowl with a plate and let it sit for 5 to 10 minutes, until the chocolate has completely melted. Sieve in the cornstarch and matcha powder, and mix until well combined. Add the eggs and whisk until smooth. Pour the batter into the lined tin and bake for 15 minutes, or until the surface is slightly set.

Meanwhile, make the chocolate layer. In a small saucepan, heat the cream and butter over medium heat for 4 minutes, or until steaming. Place the chocolate in a large heatproof bowl and pour the cream over the chocolate. Cover the bowl with a plate and let sit for 5 to 10 minutes, until the chocolate has completely melted. Sieve in the cornstarch and mix until well combined. Add the sugar and eggs, whisk until smooth and carefully pour over the par-baked matcha batter. Place the tin in a 9 x 13-inch (22 x 33-cm) rectangular pan filled with 0.8 inches (2 cm) of boiling water. Bake for 40 minutes, or until the edges are set and the center is slightly jiggly. Remove from the oven, cover and chill overnight, or for a minimum of 4 hours.

Once chilled, remove from the pan and dust with cocoa powder. Slice and serve cold with whipped cream, or heat and serve with ice cream, if using.

Reserve the cake in the fridge until it's ready to be served. The cake can be stored in an airtight container in the fridge for up to a week.

pandan chiffon cake

One of the most popular chiffon cake flavors in Southeast Asia and deemed the national cake of Singapore is pandan chiffon! Pandan is a plant native to Southeast Asia used in both sweet and savory cooking for its tropical, grassy and coconut-like flavor. Pandan extract is widely available and easy to use, but it doesn't have the same aroma as fresh pandan leaves. On the other hand, frozen pandan leaves can be found in most Asian grocery stores and, when blended with coconut milk, release a delicious aroma. Trust me, coconut and pandan paired with this light and fluffy cake will have you hooked.

makes 1 (8-inch [20-cm]) chiffon cake

½ cup (120 ml) coconut milk

10 frozen or fresh pandan leaves, roughly chopped

6 large egg yolks

⅔ cup (130 g) superfine sugar, divided

⅓ cup (80 ml) vegetable oil

1¼ cups (150 g) cake flour

2 tsp (8 g) baking powder

6 large egg whites

To make the pandan chiffon cake, preheat the oven to 340°F (170°C) and prepare an ungreased 8-inch (20-cm) chiffon cake tin with a removable base. It's important to use an ungreased cake tin as the cake uses the sides of the tin to rise.

In a blender, combine the coconut milk and pandan leaves and blitz until smooth. Pour the pandan milk through a fine-meshed sieve to extract ½ cup + 1 tablespoon (135 ml) of pandan milk. Use the back of a spoon to press the pandan leaf pulp to extract more milk. If you are short, add a splash of coconut milk to make up the missing volume.

In a medium-sized bowl, combine the egg yolks, 3 tablespoons (40 g) of sugar, vegetable oil and pandan milk, and whisk to combine. Sieve in the cake flour and baking powder, whisk until smooth and set aside.

Place the egg whites in the bowl of a stand mixer fitted with a whisk attachment and whisk on medium-high speed for 2 minutes, or until foamy. Add ⅓ cup + 2 tablespoons (90 g) of sugar and continue to whisk for 5 minutes, or until the meringue forms stiff peaks. Add one-third of the meringue to the egg yolk mixture and whisk until well combined.

Transfer the lightened egg yolk mixture to the remaining meringue and fold in gently until the batter is just combined. Slowly pour the batter into the cake tin and bake for 45 minutes, or until an inserted skewer emerges clean. Remove from the oven and invert the tin on a wire rack to remove the cake. Cool for 1 hour, or until completely cooled. Once cooled, run a thin knife around the sides and base of the cake to loosen it from the tin.

This cake is best the day it's baked, as it's at optimal fluffiness. Otherwise, store the cake in an airtight container at room temperature for up to 3 days.

I highly recommend toasting the cake the next day in a toaster oven for a couple of minutes for a warm and slightly crisp cake.

japanese–style basque cheesecake

If there has been an iconic cheesecake over the past couple of years, it's the burnt Basque cheesecake. Originating in a small bar called La Viña in San Sebastián, this slightly charred rustic cheesecake is somewhere in between a flan and a New York cheesecake without the crust. It has taken the world by storm and has been recreated over and over. Among those recreations, the Japanese-style Basque cheesecake stands out with its silky-smooth texture, slightly oozy center and smoky burnt crust. I'd go as far as to say they've made a perfect cheesecake even better. Cheesecake-lovers, this is a must-try!

makes a 6-inch (15-cm) cheesecake

16 oz (450 g) cream cheese, room temperature

¾ cup (150 g) granulated sugar

3 large eggs, room temperature

2 tbsp (15 g) cornstarch

1 tsp vanilla bean paste

¾ cup (180 ml) heavy cream

Preheat the oven to 465°F (240°C) and line a 6-inch (15-cm) cake tin with baking paper.

In the bowl of a stand mixer fitted with a paddle attachment, add the cream cheese and sugar and beat on medium speed for 3 minutes, or until smooth. Add the eggs one at a time, mixing well in between each addition. Sieve in the cornstarch and add the vanilla bean paste, then beat for 2 minutes, or until smooth. With the stand mixer on low, slowly stream in the cream and beat for 1 minute until well combined.

Pour the batter into the lined cake tin and bake for 25 minutes, or until the top is dark brown and the center is set, but soft and jiggly. Turn the heat off and wedge a wooden spoon in the oven door. Allow the cake to cool in the oven for 10 minutes, then remove from the oven, cover and chill overnight, or for a minimum of 4 hours before enjoying. The trick to the soft set center is placing the cake in the fridge straight out of the oven to cool it instantly. This won't affect your fridge, but if you're worried about your fridge becoming warm, turn it down to the coolest setting.

This cake is best enjoyed chilled; reserve the cake in the fridge until it's ready to be served. The cake can be stored in an airtight container in the fridge for up to 4 days.

coconut, lychee and raspberry lamingtons

Being raised in Australia, I grew up eating lamingtons. Whether it was a morning tea treat or bake sale cake, these chocolate-coated coconut cakes were my childhood. I guess these lamingtons are a little like me, born and raised in Australia with a Chinese background, only it's an Australian cake with an Asian twist. The coconut milk makes the sponge cake incredibly moist, and it works with the white chocolate glaze and raspberry lychee jam like a dream.

makes 12 squares

coconut and lychee cake

1 cup + 2 tbsp (270 ml) coconut milk

2 tsp (10 ml) white vinegar

3 tbsp (45 g) unsalted butter

1 cup + 2 tbsp (225 g) granulated sugar

¼ cup + 2 tbsp (90 ml) vegetable oil

3 large eggs, room temperature

2 cups (240 g) all-purpose flour

1½ tsp (6 g) baking powder

⅓ tsp baking soda

Pinch of salt

raspberry and lychee jam

1 oz (28 g) raspberries

4 oz (113 g) pitted lychees, roughly chopped

2 tbsp (25 g) granulated sugar

1 tsp lemon juice

To make the coconut and lychee cake, preheat the oven to 350°F (180°C) and line a 9 x 13–inch (22 x 33–cm) rectangular pan with baking paper. Combine the coconut milk and vinegar in a small bowl, and set aside. Meanwhile, in the bowl of a stand mixer fitted with a paddle attachment, combine the butter, sugar and oil and beat on medium-high for 5 minutes, or until light and fluffy. Add the eggs and beat on high for 3 minutes until well combined.

In a medium-sized bowl, combine the flour, baking powder, baking soda and salt, whisk to combine and add half of the mixture to the stand mixer containing the combined butter, sugar, oil and eggs. Beat on low speed for 1 minute, or until just combined. With the mixer running on low, add the coconut milk and mix until just combined. Add the remaining half of the mixture of flour, baking powder, baking soda and salt, and beat until just incorporated. Transfer the batter to the lined tin and bake for 30 minutes, or until an inserted toothpick emerges clean. Remove from the oven and cool for 1 hour or until completely cool.

Meanwhile, prepare the raspberry and lychee jam. In a small saucepan over medium-high heat, combine the raspberries, lychees, sugar and lemon juice, and cook for 5 to 6 minutes, stirring occasionally, until the fruit has broken down and thickened. Remove from the heat and cool for 1 hour or until completely cool.

Once the jam and cake have cooled completely, prepare the lamingtons for assembly. Trim the top and edges of the cake to create a flat and even layer. Cut the cake in half horizontally and spread the jam over one half. Top with the other half and cut into twelve squares.

(continued)

coconut, lychee and raspberry lamingtons *(continued)*

glaze

2 oz (56 g) raspberries

4 oz (113 g) pitted lychees

¼ cup + 2 tbsp (90 ml) heavy cream

7 oz (200 g) white chocolate, melted

3 cups (280 g) desiccated coconut, for dusting

To make the glaze, blitz the raspberries, lychees and cream in a blender until smooth. Pour into a shallow bowl and add the melted white chocolate. Mix until well combined. Place the coconut in another shallow bowl and set it aside.

Prepare a wire rack for the lamingtons to set on. Dip the cake squares into the glaze, then into the coconut to coat. Place the completed lamingtons on the wire rack and continue until all the cakes have been coated. Allow the lamingtons to set for 30 minutes before enjoying.

These are best consumed at room temperature, but they can be stored in an airtight container in the fridge for up to 3 days. Allow them to sit at room temperature for 15 minutes before consuming.

molten hojicha dulce de leche lava cakes

Here's a collaboration between Japanese and Latin American cuisine! Hojicha (焙じ茶), or roasted green tea, is a mellow, nutty and fragrant tea originating in Japan that is becoming increasingly popular, particularly in desserts. Dulce de leche is loved all around the world because of its creamy caramelized taste. When paired, these two very different flavors create a completely new experience. This is my take on the classic chocolate fondant, but instead of a molten chocolate center, you'll cut this tender cake open to reveal a puddle of warm and decadent hojicha caramel.

makes 3 (4-oz [115-g]) cakes

special equipment

3 (4-oz [115-ml]) dariole molds or ramekins

dulce de leche

1 (14-oz [395-g]) can of condensed milk, or store-bought dulce de leche

cake

Butter, to grease the molds

All-purpose flour, to dust the molds

2 large egg yolks

1 large egg

1 tbsp (8 g) all-purpose flour

2 tbsp (12 g) hojicha powder

assembly

Ice cream or whipped cream

Hojicha powder, for dusting

To make the dulce de leche, place the can of condensed milk in a pot of water, ensuring the can is completely covered. Bring the water to a gentle simmer and cook for 4 hours, then turn off the heat and allow the can to cool completely in the pot. Make sure to top the water up throughout the cooking process; otherwise, your can might explode.

To make the cakes, preheat the oven to 390°F (200°C). Grease three large dariole molds with butter and dust with flour, tapping out any excess. If you don't have the perfect molds, use whatever you have on hand, such as mugs or ramekins. Keep an eye on the cakes and respectively increase or decrease the cook time by 1 to 2 minutes, if using a larger or smaller mold. Bake until the cakes are barely set in the center.

In a large bowl, add the egg yolks, egg and dulce de leche, and whisk to combine. Sieve in the flour and hojicha powder, and whisk until just combined. Carefully pour the batter into the prepared molds, stopping 10 mm from the brim. Place the molds on a baking tray and bake for 8 minutes, or until the surface of the cake is set with a soft center. Invert onto your serving plate and tap the base to carefully unmold. Serve with a scoop of ice cream or whipped cream and a dusting of hojicha powder.

These cakes must be eaten immediately to enjoy the molten center. If you're preparing them in advance, place the filled molds in the fridge and bake for 10 minutes before serving.

japanese soufflé cheesecake

Japan is known for its soufflé cheesecakes. Unlike regular cheesecakes that are dense, rich and creamy, these are soufflé-like and melt in your mouth. The dreamy texture is created by folding a meringue through the cream cheese batter and baking it in a bain-marie, or hot water bath. When enjoyed warm, the cake is wobbly with a taste closer to a sponge cake, and when cooled, the cream cheese flavor deepens for a super-light cheesecake. Try both and see what you prefer!

makes an 8-inch (20-cm) cake

10.5 oz (300 g) cream cheese, room temperature

2 tbsp (30 g) unsalted butter, cubed, room temperature

⅓ cup (80 ml) whole milk

5 large eggs, yolks and whites separated

⅓ cup + 3 tbsp (103 g) granulated sugar, divided

½ cup + 1 tbsp (70 g) cake flour

To make the cheesecake, preheat the oven to 320°F (160°C) and line the base of an 8-inch (20-cm) cake tin with baking paper. There is no need to grease the sides of the pan, as the sides will act as a wall on which the sponge batter can climb. This results in a taller and fluffier cake.

Bring a small saucepan of water to a boil, then reduce to a simmer. In a heatproof bowl slightly larger than the saucepan, combine the cream cheese, butter and milk. Place the bowl over the saucepan and gently heat for 5 minutes, whisking until smooth. Remove the bowl from the saucepan and add the egg yolks and 3 tablespoons (38 g) of sugar. Whisk to combine. Sieve in the cake flour and whisk until smooth.

In the bowl of a stand mixer fitted with a whisk attachment, beat the egg whites on medium-high for 2 minutes, or until foamy. Add ⅓ cup (65 g) of sugar and continue to whisk for 5 minutes, or until the meringue forms stiff peaks. Fold one-third of the meringue into the egg yolk mixture and whisk until smooth. Transfer the lightened egg yolk mixture to the remaining meringue and fold gently until the batter is just combined. Slowly pour the batter into the lined tin and bake for 1 hour, or until the top is golden brown. Turn the heat off, wedge a wooden spoon in the oven door and allow the cake to cool in the oven for 1 hour.

Once cooled, run a thin knife along the sides of the pan to release the sides. Invert the pan to unmold the cake and remove the attached baking paper.

Enjoy this cake warm for a fluffy texture, or chill overnight for a cheesier, firmer cake. The cake can be stored in an airtight container in the fridge for up to 4 days.

paper-wrapped chiffon cupcakes

Paper-wrapped chiffon cupcakes (港式纸包蛋糕) are a Hong Kong bakery classic that can be found in every Chinese bakery. These light and slightly eggy cupcakes are baked in tall flower-shaped tins to create the iconic cupcake shape and texture with a caramelized crust. The tall cupcake tins help the batter climb up the walls to create an extremely light sponge; however, these tins aren't widely available and are hard to source. An easy substitute that works just as well are paper cups! Line some paper cups with baking paper and bake these chiffon cupcakes for an easy pillowy treat.

makes 6 (8-oz [225-g]) cupcakes

special equipment

6 (8-oz [225-g]) paper cups or a tall 6-cavity cupcake tin

cupcakes

3 large eggs, yolks and whites separated

2 tbsp + 1 tsp (35 ml) whole milk

2 tbsp (30 ml) vegetable oil

1 tsp vanilla bean paste

½ cup (62 g) cake flour

¼ cup (50 g) granulated sugar

Preheat the oven to 350°F (180°C) and line six paper cups with baking paper. To line each cup perfectly, place an 8-inch (20-cm) square of baking paper on top of one cup. Push another cup down onto the baking paper and into the first cup, as though you are stacking the cups.

To make the batter, combine the egg yolks, milk, oil and vanilla bean paste in a medium-sized mixing bowl and whisk until combined. Sieve in the cake flour, whisk until just combined and set aside.

In the bowl of a stand mixer fitted with a whisk attachment, beat the egg whites on medium-high for 2 minutes, or until foamy. Add the sugar and continue to whisk for 5 minutes, or until the meringue forms stiff peaks. Fold one-third of the meringue into the egg yolk mixture and whisk until smooth. Transfer the lightened egg yolk mixture to the remaining meringue and fold gently until the batter is just combined.

Transfer the batter to a piping bag and snip off a large opening. Carefully fill the lined paper cups with batter and bake for 25 to 30 minutes, or until the cakes are golden brown. Remove from the oven and immediately lay the cups on their sides. This prevents the cakes from shrinking too much. Cool for 30 minutes, then remove the cakes from the cups and enjoy.

These cakes are best the day they're baked as they are at optimal fluffiness. Otherwise, store the cakes in an airtight container at room temperature for up to 3 days.

I highly recommend toasting the cakes the next day in a toaster oven for a couple of minutes for a warm and slightly crisp cake.

the cookie collection

Cookies were one of the first things I tackled on my baking journey because of how easy they are to make. Even now I'll turn to a good cookie recipe when I'm looking for something to bake! In some ways, this chapter reflects my own journey through cookies. There are easy one-bowl cookies that are perfect for beginners. Then we've got sandwich cookies which take a little more time and effort, and once you've mastered all of those, we've got . . . macarons!

Macarons have an infamous reputation for being tricky little cookies. The process doesn't seem that difficult, but small deviations from the recipe can cause major problems: flat cookies, hollow shells, cracked tops, sticky bottoms . . . and the list goes on. Mastering macarons was a huge step for me on my baking journey, and I wanted to share that with all of you. The sense of accomplishment you feel once you create the perfect macaron is something you have to experience!

From constructing a macaron tower in front of the macaron master Adriano Zumbo to writing an entire e-book on the cookie, and even starting and closing my own macaron business, these cookies and I have a long history. Over the years, I've collected my own tips and created an easy and fool-proof method to perfect the macaron shell. I've taken out the unnecessary steps and details, so with practice, you'll be creating the macarons of your dreams!

This chapter brings you a mix of my favorite cookies, and I hope I can introduce some exciting flavors, techniques and textures to your kitchen. There are buttery, shortbread-like Chocolate Matcha Viennese Swirls (page 106), soft Miso Chocolate Chunk Cookies (page 97), crispy Yuzu Cheesecake Macarons (page 94), Black Sesame Praline Macarons (page 98), chewy Black Sesame Brownie Cookies (page 105) and more. With the invention of Matcha Mochi Cookies (page 90), we've even got the combination of crunchy, soft and chewy! The possibilities are endless, and it's your turn to explore them.

matcha mochi cookies

Mochi has taken over the baking world and made its way into our everyday bakes. This cookie is flavored with matcha, finely ground green tea powder, to create a buttery, fragrant and sweet cookie that pulls apart to reveal a stretchy chewy treat made of glutinous rice flour. With all the different textures, you'll never get bored of this cookie.

makes 10 cookies

mochi

½ cup (65 g) glutinous rice flour

1 tbsp (13 g) granulated sugar

½ cup (120 ml) whole milk

1 tbsp (15 g) unsalted butter, room temperature

cookie

½ cup (120 g) unsalted butter, room temperature

½ cup (90 g) brown sugar, unpacked

1 large egg, room temperature

1½ cups (180 g) all-purpose flour

1 tsp baking powder

1 tbsp (6 g) matcha powder

Pinch of salt

assembly

3 oz (85 g) compound white chocolate or candy melts

Matcha powder, for dusting

To make the mochi, combine the glutinous rice flour, sugar and milk in a microwave-safe bowl, and whisk until smooth. Cover the bowl with cling wrap and use a fork to poke several holes. This allows built-up steam to escape while cooking. Microwave on high for 2 minutes, before removing and mixing to incorporate any raw areas of dough. Re-cover the bowl and microwave for 1-minute bursts, until the mochi dough is semi-translucent and no longer milky. This should take a total of 3 to 4 minutes. Keep covered and cool for 30 minutes, or until cool enough to handle.

Line a baking tray with baking paper. Once the mochi has cooled, add the butter. Using gloved or oiled hands, knead the cooled mochi dough until smooth and stretchy. Kneading the dough helps incorporate the butter while enhancing the mochi's chewy texture. Divide the mochi into ten equal balls and place them on the prepared tray.

To make the cookies, cream the butter and brown sugar in a stand mixer fitted with the paddle attachment on medium-high speed for 4 minutes, or until smooth and lightened. Add the egg and beat for 1 minute, or until combined. Sieve in the flour, baking powder, matcha powder and salt, and beat on low speed for another minute, or until just combined. Cover the bowl with cling wrap and chill for 1 hour, or until firm. This prevents the cookies from spreading when baking.

Once the dough has chilled, preheat the oven to 355 °F (180°C). Line a baking tray with baking paper. Divide the cookie dough into ten equal portions. Roll each portion into a ball and flatten it between your palms. Place a ball of mochi in the center of the flattened dough and bring the sides together to enclose the mochi. Place the mochi cookie on the prepared tray and repeat with the remaining portions, leaving 2 inches (5 cm) in between to prevent them from spreading into each other. Bake for 10 to 11 minutes, or until matte and set. Cool for 30 minutes, or until cooled completely.

To assemble, melt the compound white chocolate and drizzle it over the cookies. Dust the cookies with matcha powder to serve!

Compound white chocolate sets hard at room temperature without tempering. If you don't have any on hand, feel free to use regular white chocolate, but keep in mind the chocolate won't set as well.

These cookies are best consumed the day they are made. Mochi tends to go stale and lose its soft, chewy texture after 1 to 2 days, so eat them fresh!

miso alfajores

This is my adaption of the classic alfajor, one of my favorite cookies and one with such a deep history. Originating in the Middle East, then Spain and now immensely popularized in South America, this classic has inspired so many variations. There is nothing you can't love about a sweet and crumbly melt-in-your-mouth cookie, and that extra touch of miso brings a slightly savory, salty tone to a perfect caramel treat.

makes 18 alfajores

miso dulce de leche

1 (14-oz [395-g]) can condensed milk, or store-bought dulce de leche

2 tbsp (35 g) white miso paste

cookies

1 cup (235 g) unsalted butter, softened

⅔ cup (75 g) powdered sugar

4 large egg yolks

2 tsp (10 ml) vanilla extract

2 cups (250 g) cornstarch

1½ cups (180 g) all-purpose flour

1 tsp baking powder

To make the miso dulce de leche, place the can of condensed milk in a pot of water, ensuring the can is completely covered. Bring the water to a gentle simmer and cook for 4 hours, then turn off the heat and allow the can to cool completely in the pot. Make sure to top the water up throughout the cooking process; otherwise, your can might explode.

In the bowl of a stand mixer fitted with a paddle attachment, combine the cooled can of dulce de leche and miso paste. Beat on low speed for 3 minutes, or until completely smooth. Transfer to a piping bag fitted with a medium-sized round tip.

To make the cookies, cream the butter and sugar in a stand mixer fitted with a paddle attachment on medium speed for 4 minutes, or until smooth. Add the egg yolks and vanilla extract and beat for another 2 minutes, or until smooth. Add the cornstarch, flour and baking powder, and beat on low speed until just combined. Place the dough between two large sheets of baking paper and roll to 5 mm in thickness. Place the dough on a baking tray and chill for 1 hour, or until firm.

Once the dough has chilled, preheat the oven to 345°F (175°C). Line a baking tray with baking paper. Remove the upper layer of baking paper and cut out rounds of dough using a 2-inch (5-cm) round cookie cutter. Place the cut-out rounds on the prepared tray, leaving 2 inches (5 cm) in between to prevent them from spreading into each other. Gather the scraps and roll them out between the same two sheets of baking paper to cut out more cookies for a total of about 36 cookies.

Bake the cookies for 10 to 12 minutes, until the cookies are set but pale in color. Cool completely and match similar-sized cookies together. Pipe a dollop of miso dulce de leche on the bottom of one cookie and top with the matching cookie.

Let these cookies sit for 1 to 2 hours before consuming. This allows the cookie to absorb the delicious dulce de leche flavor. Store in an airtight container in the fridge for up to a week.

yuzu cheesecake macarons

Yuzu (柚子), yuja (유자) or xiāngchéng (香橙) is a citrus originating in Southeast Asia known for its unique flavor and fragrance. The fruit itself is sour, slightly bitter and very fragrant, perfect for baking! Although fresh yuzu may be difficult to find, bottled yuzu juice is available from most Asian grocery stores. Add a splash to this cream cheese filling to create a unique, tangy cheesecake-inspired macaron.

makes 18 macarons

macaron shells

1 batch French Macaron Shells (page 12)

Yellow gel food coloring

yuzu cheesecake filling

6 oz (175 g) cream cheese, room temperature

⅓ cup (80 g) unsalted butter, room temperature

¼ cup (50 g) granulated sugar

1 tbsp (15 ml) yuzu juice

Prepare the macaron shells as per the French Macaron Shells recipe (page 12), using yellow food coloring.

To make the yuzu cheesecake filling, combine the cream cheese, butter, sugar and yuzu juice in the bowl of a stand mixer fitted with a whisk attachment, and whisk on medium speed for 5 minutes, or until smooth and creamy. Transfer the cream to a piping bag fitted with a large round tip and set aside.

Once the shells have cooled, match similar-sized macaron shells together. Pipe a dollop of yuzu cheesecake filling on the bottom of one shell and top with the matching shell. Place the macarons in an airtight container in the fridge for 2 to 3 hours to mature.

Maturing the macarons allows the shells to take on the flavor and moisture of the filling, creating a flavorful, chewy cookie. Macarons usually take up to 1 day to mature, but the moisture in the yuzu filling speeds up the process.

Keep these refrigerated in an airtight container and enjoy within 2 days.

miso chocolate chunk cookies

These are my ultimate chocolate chip cookies! When you think of miso, you might think of that delicious soup served with your Japanese food, but trust me, this savory fermented bean paste does wonders for cookies. The miso complements the brown butter and caramelized sugars for a perfectly balanced treat.

makes 9 cookies

½ cup (120 g) unsalted butter, cubed

2 tbsp (35 g) white miso paste

1⅔ cups (200 g) all-purpose flour

½ tsp baking powder

½ tsp baking soda

½ cup (90 g) brown sugar, unpacked

⅓ cup (65 g) granulated sugar

1 large egg

1 large egg yolk

3.5 oz (100 g) dark chocolate, roughly chopped

Flakey salt, for sprinkling

To make the cookies, place the butter in a small saucepan over medium heat for 3 minutes, or until melted. Continue to heat the butter, swirling the pan occasionally, for 3 to 5 minutes, until browned and fragrant. You will notice toasted milk solids on the bottom of the pan. Remove from the heat and mix in the miso paste, stir until melted and set aside.

Meanwhile, in a large mixing bowl, combine the flour, baking powder and baking soda. Whisk to combine. Add the brown sugar, granulated sugar, egg and egg yolk to the cooled brown butter, and whisk until combined. Fold in the chopped dark chocolate, cover with cling wrap and chill for 1 hour, or until firm.

To bake the cookies, preheat the oven to 350°F (180°C) and line one large or two small baking trays with baking paper. Roll the cookie dough into nine equal balls and place them on the baking tray, leaving 2 inches (5 cm) in between to prevent them from spreading into each other. Bake for 13 to 15 minutes until lightly golden brown. Cool for 15 minutes. Sprinkle with the flakey salt to enjoy!

Store the cookies in an airtight container at room temperature for up to 4 days.

black sesame praline macarons

If you are a fan of black sesame, these are an absolute must! The praline creates an intense caramelized black sesame flavor that is balanced by the creamy French buttercream. The process is a little labor-intensive; however, the result is so worth it. These were a bestseller when I ran my small business and have stuck with me ever since!

makes 18 macarons

macaron shells

1 batch French Macaron Shells (page 12)

Black gel food coloring

black sesame praline

¼ cup (50 g) granulated sugar

⅓ cup (50 g) black sesame seeds

3 tbsp (45 ml) vegetable oil

french buttercream

3 tbsp (45 ml) whole milk

2 large egg yolks

2 tbsp (25 g) granulated sugar

⅔ cup (150 g) unsalted butter, room temperature

1 tbsp (15 ml) black sesame praline

Prepare the macarons as per the French Macaron Shells recipe (page 12), using black food coloring.

To make the black sesame praline, heat the sugar in a small saucepan over medium heat for 4 minutes, or until golden brown in color. Add the black sesame seeds and mix until just combined. Transfer the black sesame caramel to a sheet of baking paper and cool completely. Break the set caramel into large chunks and place them in a blender. Process until a fine powder, then add the oil and continue to process until a smooth paste forms. This process can take up to 10 minutes. Reserve 1 tablespoon (15 ml) of praline and transfer the remaining paste to a piping bag. Set it aside until the macarons are ready to be filled.

To make the buttercream, make a custard by heating the milk in a small saucepan over medium heat for 3 minutes, or until steaming. Meanwhile, in a medium-sized heatproof bowl, combine the egg yolks and sugar and whisk to combine. Slowly pour the steaming milk into the egg yolks, whisking continuously until well combined. Return the mixture to the saucepan and whisk constantly over low heat for 3 to 4 minutes, until thickened. It should be thick enough to hold a line when a utensil is drawn across the base of the pot. Transfer to a small bowl and cool for 30 minutes, or until room temperature.

Once the custard has cooled, place the room temperature butter into the bowl of a stand mixer fitted with a whisk attachment. Whisk the butter on medium speed for 3 minutes, or until smooth, then add the cooled custard and reserved of black sesame praline paste. Continue to beat the buttercream for 5 minutes, or until light and fluffy. Transfer to a piping bag fitted with a medium-sized round piping tip and set aside.

To assemble the macarons, match similar-sized macaron shells together. Pipe a ring of French buttercream on the bottom of one shell. Add a dollop of black sesame praline to the center and top with the matching shell.

Chill the filled macarons in an airtight container overnight, or for a minimum of 6 hours, to allow the macarons to mature. Maturing the macarons allows the shells to take on the flavor and moisture of the filling, creating a flavorful, chewy cookie. Keep these refrigerated in an airtight container and consume them within 3 days.

tahini "nutter butters"

These tahini sandwich cookies are my take on "Nutter Butters" with an Asian twist: rich and buttery oat cookies with a sweet sesame buttercream. Tahini is a staple in Asian cooking because of its nutty fragrance, and sesame seeds are commonly used in Chinese sweets. You can see these as Americanized Chinese sesame cookies, which are the best of both worlds. Unhulled tahini is the most widely available sesame paste available from Asian grocery stores; however, hulled tahini will work just as well!

makes 15 "Nutter Butters"

tahini cookie

¾ cup (180 g) unsalted butter, room temperature

½ cup (90 g) brown sugar, unpacked

½ cup (120 g) tahini, hulled or unhulled

1 large egg

1 tsp vanilla extract

1½ cups (180 g) all-purpose flour

1 tsp baking powder

1 cup (90 g) rolled oats

¼ cup (38 g) sesame seeds

tahini buttercream

¼ cup (60 g) unsalted butter, room temperature

⅓ cup (80 g) tahini, hulled or unhulled

½ cup (50 g) powdered sugar

¼ tsp salt

To make the tahini cookies, combine the butter, brown sugar and tahini in the bowl of a stand mixer fitted with a paddle attachment, and beat on medium speed for 4 minutes, or until light and fluffy. Add the egg and vanilla extract, and continue to beat for 2 minutes, or until combined. Sieve in the flour and baking powder, and mix until just combined. Fold in the oats and sesame seeds, then cover and chill for 30 minutes, or until firm.

To bake the cookies, preheat the oven to 325°F (160°C) and line one large or two small baking trays with baking paper. Remove the chilled dough and roll into 30 equally sized balls. Place the balls on the tray or trays, leaving 2 inches (5 cm) in between to prevent them from spreading into each other. Flatten them slightly with your palm and bake for 15 to 16 minutes, until golden brown. Remove from the oven and cool for 1 hour, or until completely cool before filling.

To make the buttercream, combine the butter, tahini, powdered sugar and salt in the bowl of a stand mixer fitted with a paddle attachment and beat on medium-high for 5 minutes, or until light and fluffy. Transfer the buttercream to a piping bag fitted with a large round tip.

To assemble, match similar-sized cookies together. Pipe a dollop of tahini buttercream on the bottom of one cookie and top with the matching cookie.

Store in an airtight container in the fridge for up to a week. Let the cookies sit at room temperature for 5 minutes before enjoying!

ube crinkles

These ube crinkles are a Filipino take on the popular crinkle cookie. I've replaced the traditional cocoa powder with ube halaya and extract for a nutty vanilla-like flavor and stunning purple hue. While crinkle cookies might be a popular holiday baking project, these fudgy ube crinkles with their crunchy, crackled exterior are delicious no matter the time of the year.

makes 10 crinkles

cookie dough

1¾ cups (210 g) all-purpose flour

½ cup (100 g) granulated sugar

1 tsp baking powder

½ cup (120 g) unsalted butter, melted

1 large egg

½ cup (113 g) ube halaya

1 tsp ube extract

assembly

Superfine sugar, for rolling

Powdered sugar, for rolling

To make the cookies, combine the flour, sugar and baking powder in a mixing bowl, and whisk until combined. Mix in the melted butter, egg, ube halaya and ube extract. Cover the bowl with cling wrap and chill for 30 minutes, or until firm.

Once chilled, roll the dough into ten balls and freeze for 1 hour, or until solid.

To bake the cookies, preheat the oven to 350°F (180°C). Line a baking tray with baking paper. Remove the cookie dough from the freezer and roll each ball in superfine sugar, then powdered sugar, ensuring the dough is well coated. Place the coated balls on the prepared tray, leaving 2 inches (5 cm) in between to prevent them from spreading into each other, and bake for 15 minutes or until set. Remove from the oven and cool for 30 minutes, or until completely cool.

Store the cookies in an airtight container at room temperature for up to 4 days.

black sesame brownie cookies

If brownies and cookies were to have a child, this would be it. These cookies are the embodiment of a fudgy brownie with a slightly crisp exterior, all the best bits in one treat. The added black sesame adds another layer of complexity, enhancing the cookies' texture and flavor for the perfect chocolatey bite.

makes 12 cookies

8 oz (225 g) dark chocolate, 70% cocoa, roughly chopped

¼ cup (60 g) unsalted butter, cubed

⅔ cup (80 g) all-purpose flour

1 tsp baking powder

2 tbsp (15 g) cocoa powder

3 tbsp (27 g) black sesame seeds

¼ tsp salt

2 large eggs

⅔ cup (130 g) superfine sugar

½ cup (90 g) brown sugar, unpacked

Mixed sesame seeds, for sprinkling

To make the cookies, preheat the oven to 340°F (170°C) and line one large or two small baking trays with baking paper. These cookies are time and temperature-sensitive, so make sure that you have all the ingredients ready to go. The more the melted chocolate cools the less prominent the crinkle effect on the cookies will be.

Melt the chocolate and butter in a heatproof bowl over a pan of boiling water, or in the microwave in 30-second intervals. Remove and set aside. Meanwhile, in a medium-sized bowl, combine the flour, baking powder, cocoa powder, black sesame seeds and salt, and whisk until free of lumps. In the bowl of a stand mixer fitted with a whisk attachment, combine the eggs, superfine sugar and brown sugar, and beat on medium-high for 8 to 10 minutes, until light, fluffy and doubled in volume. Add the chocolate mixture to the eggs and whisk for 2 minutes, or until combined. Then fold in the mixture of flour, baking powder, cocoa powder, black sesame seeds and salt until just combined.

Using a cookie scoop or spoon, scoop 2-tablespoon (40-g) rounds of cookie batter onto the lined baking tray or trays. The batter will be soft and difficult to handle, so the best way to shape your cookies is with a cookie scoop or ice cream scoop. If you don't have one, use a spoon to scoop the batter and another spoon to help ease the batter onto the tray. Sprinkle the cookies with mixed sesame seeds and bake for 13 to 15 minutes until the cookies are cracked and set. Cool for 1 hour, or until completely cool.

Store the cookies in an airtight container at room temperature for up to 5 days.

chocolate matcha viennese swirls

Viennese whirls were one of my favorite cookies growing up! I'm a fan of anything with a shortbread-like texture and these are so short that they barely hold themselves together. Chocolate and matcha are a match-a made in heaven and work perfectly in these cookies. If you're feeling extra fancy, dip these in dark chocolate for the ultimate chocolate-covered shortbread.

makes 15 swirls

½ cup (120 g) unsalted butter, room temperature

1 cup (120 g) all-purpose flour

¼ cup (30 g) cornstarch

⅓ cup (35 g) powdered sugar

2 tsp (4 g) matcha powder

1 tbsp (15 g) cocoa powder

To make the cookies, preheat the oven to 320°F (160°C) and line one large or two small baking trays with baking paper.

In the bowl of a stand mixer fitted with a paddle attachment, beat the butter on medium-high for 3 minutes, or until smooth. Reduce the speed to low and add the flour, cornstarch and sugar, and beat for 2 minutes, until a dough forms. Place half of this cookie dough into a separate bowl and add the matcha powder. Mix until just combined and transfer to a piping bag. Add the cocoa powder to the other half of the cookie dough. Mix until just combined and transfer to another piping bag. Cut a 10-mm opening from the tip of both piping bags and place both of them together into another piping bag fitted with a large star nozzle.

Using a firm grip, pipe the combined matcha and chocolate cookie dough into swirls on the lined baking tray or trays, leaving 2 inches (5 cm) in between to prevent them from spreading into each other. Bake for 15 minutes, or until the cookies are set. They may appear soft when hot, but they will firm up when cooled. Cool for 30 minutes, or until completely cooled, before enjoying.

Store the cookies in an airtight container at room temperature for up to a week.

strawberry milk "fatcarons"

"Fatcarons," or ddungcaron (뚱카롱), are South Korea's take on the French macaron. Usually enjoyed chilled for a chewier texture, these are filled with a thick layer of light buttercream to live up to their name. While the extra cream may make the macarons look heavy and hard to eat, it actually adds a lightness to the cookies, which are usually filled with sweeter fillings like jams and ganaches. These cute pink macarons are like a bite of sweet and creamy strawberry milk with a tangy strawberry jam center!

makes 18 "fatcarons"

macaron shells

1 batch French Macaron Shells (page 12)

Pink gel food coloring

strawberry jam

4 oz (115 g) strawberries, roughly chopped

2 tbsp (25 g) granulated sugar

strawberry italian meringue buttercream

White vinegar, to wipe down the bowl

4 tbsp (60 g) egg whites, approx. 2 large egg whites

½ cup (100 g) granulated sugar

¼ cup (60 ml) water

½ cup (120 g) unsalted butter, room temperature, sliced into tablespoons

2 tbsp (40 g) prepared strawberry jam

Prepare the macarons as per the French Macaron Shells recipe (page 12), using pink food coloring.

To make the strawberry jam, combine the strawberries and sugar in a small saucepan over medium heat. Heat, stirring occasionally, for 8 to 10 minutes until the strawberries have broken down and thickened. Remove from the heat and cool for 1 hour, or until completely cooled. Reserve 2 tablespoons (40 g) of jam. Transfer the remaining jam to a piping bag and set it aside.

To make the strawberry Italian meringue buttercream, soak a paper towel with a little white vinegar and wipe down the bowl of a stand mixer before adding the egg whites. This ensures that the egg whites whip up to a stable meringue. Fix the bowl to a stand mixer fitted with a whisk attachment and set aside until the sugar syrup is ready.

Add the sugar and water to a small saucepan over medium heat and heat for 8 to 10 minutes, until the sugar dissolves and reaches 233°F (112°C). Quickly turn your stand mixer to medium-high and start beating the egg whites. When the syrup reaches 240°F (115°C) remove the pan from the heat. Reduce the stand mixer speed to medium and pour the sugar syrup into the egg whites in a slow and steady stream. Increase the speed to high and beat for 5 minutes, or until the meringue forms stiff peaks. Then reduce the speed to medium and beat for 10 to 15 minutes, until the meringue has cooled to room temperature.

Once the meringue has cooled, increase the speed to high and add the room temperature butter 1 tablespoon (15 g) at a time. It is important that the meringue has cooled completely before adding the butter; otherwise, the buttercream may split. Once all the butter has been added, continue to whisk the buttercream for 10 to 15 minutes, or until light and silky. At this point the buttercream may curdle. That's completely normal; just keep beating and it will come back together. Fold in 2 tablespoons (40 g) of strawberry jam and transfer to a piping bag fitted with a large-sized round piping tip and set aside. If the buttercream curdles and won't come back together, place the bowl in the fridge for 15 minutes for the buttercream to firm up before continuing to whip.

(continued)

To assemble the macarons, match similar-sized macaron shells together. On the bottom of one shell pipe a tall mound of buttercream. Cut the tip of the piping bag filled with strawberry jam and insert it into the top center of the buttercream mound. Carefully squeeze the piping bag to fill the buttercream with strawberry jam and top with the matching shell.

Chill the filled macarons in an airtight container overnight, or for a minimum of 6 hours, to allow the macarons to mature. Maturing the macarons allows the shells to take on the flavor and moisture of the filling, creating a flavorful, chewy cookie.

These Korean-style macarons are best enjoyed chilled, which gives the buttercream an ice cream–like texture while the shells remain chewy. Keep these refrigerated in an airtight container and consume them within 3 days.

palmier carré

These palmiers are different from the traditional French palmier. Originating in South Korea, these are shaped like large rectangles and dipped in a thin coating of chocolate. South Korea is known for its café culture, and its bakeries are producing new and trendy desserts all the time. Palmiers are just one of the pastries that have surged in popularity, and with good reason. Who can resist layers of buttery caramelized puff pastry and chocolate?

makes 8 palmiers

rough puff pastry

1½ cups (180 g) all-purpose flour

¾ cup (180 g) unsalted butter, chilled and roughly chopped

3 tbsp (45 ml) water, iced

1 cup (200 g) granulated sugar, for rolling

To make the rough puff pastry, combine the flour and butter in a large bowl. Using your fingertips, roughly work the butter into the flour, leaving some large pea-sized chunks. The chunks of butter don't have to be even; leave some larger and smaller fragments. These chunks of butter will form the layers of pastry. Add the water and work the dough into a rough ball. Place the dough between two sheets of baking paper and roll into an 8 x 12–inch (20 x 30–cm) rectangle [1]. Transfer the dough to a baking tray and chill for 30 minutes, or until firm.

Remove from the fridge. With the long side of the rectangle facing you, visually divide the rectangle into vertical thirds [2]. Fold the two outer thirds over the center third [3]. This is a single fold. Roll the folded dough out to an 8 x 12–inch (20 x 30–cm) rectangle and perform another single fold. Wrap the dough in cling wrap and chill for 30 minutes, or until firm.

Once chilled, unwrap the dough and perform another single fold. Then, roll the dough out to an 8 x 12–inch (20 x 30–cm) rectangle [4]. With the long side of the rectangle facing you, visually divide the rectangle into fourths [5]. Fold the two outer fourths towards the centerline [6], then fold in half [7]. This is a double fold. Trim the two short uneven edges of the folded rectangle and cut the dough into thirds to create three short rectangles. Brush water on top of one rectangle and set a second on top. Brush more water on top of the second rectangle and stack the third rectangle on top. The water in between the layers will help them stick. You should now have a stack of three rectangles. Wrap the stack in cling wrap and chill for 1 to 2 hours, until firm.

To bake the palmiers, preheat the oven to 350°F (180°C) and line a large baking tray with baking paper. Place the sugar on a plate. Remove the dough from the fridge [7]. Using a sharp knife, cut 10-mm slices of dough [8] and coat them in the sugar [9]. Place the dough pieces 3 inches (8 cm) apart on the prepared tray and bake for 20 to 25 minutes until golden brown and crisp. Remove from the oven and cool. These palmiers will spread a lot as they bake, so make sure there is enough space in between each cookie.

(continued)

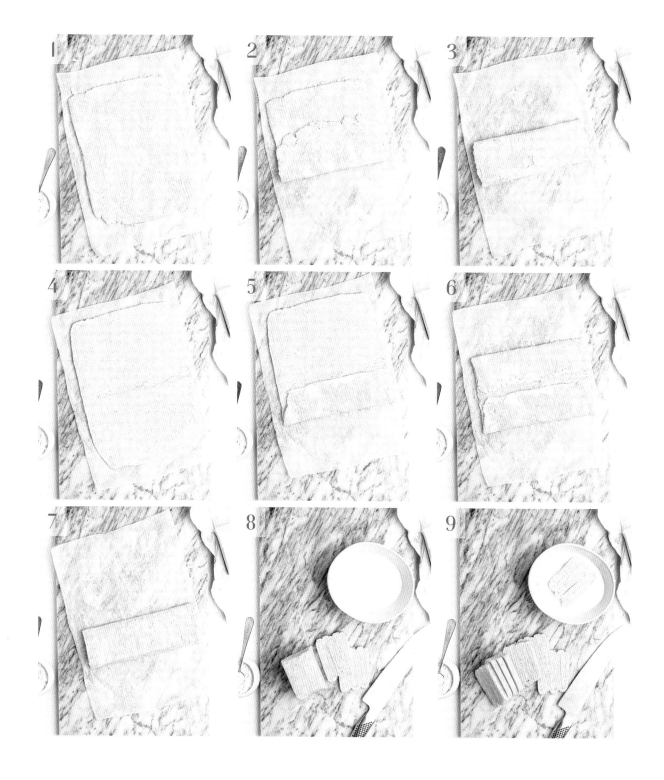

palmier carré *(continued)*

chocolate coating

7 oz (200 g) high-quality chocolate of your choice, finely chopped

While the palmiers are cooling, prepare the chocolate coating. Bring a small saucepan of water to a boil, then reduce to a simmer. Place half the chocolate in a heatproof bowl slightly larger than the saucepan. Place the bowl over the saucepan and heat gently for 5 minutes, stirring occasionally, until the chocolate has just melted. Remove from the heat and add the other half of the chocolate, stirring until completely melted. It is important to melt the chocolate in two additions, as this helps the chocolate set at room temperature.

Line a baking tray with baking paper. Dip the cooled palmiers vertically halfway into the chocolate, so that their top halves are coated, and place them on the prepared tray. Leave the cookies to set for 30 minutes at room temperature, then 30 minutes in the fridge.

Palmiers are best enjoyed on the day they're made, as their texture is still crisp and flakey. Store any remaining palmiers in an airtight container at room temperature for up to 3 days.

(For an image of this recipe, see page 172.)

buttery tarts and pastries

Tarts and pastries are arguably the best kinds of desserts because they have the best of all textures. From crisp and buttery tart shells to crunchy choux pastries and tender crêpes, from custard to caramel and fresh fruit fillings, there are so many varieties.

Once you have the basic tart shell or pastry recipe nailed, the potential is never-ending. I've made sure to pick a selection of my favorites while covering all the essentials! Whether you are looking for chocolate, caramel, ganache-filled, custard, fruity or cream-filled, I've got them all. On top of that, we've got a couple of Asian classics and choux pastries to cover the rest of the pastry realm.

Take this chapter as a guide and mix and match across recipes! Change up the banana in the Miso Caramel Banoffee Tartlets (page 125) for Pastry Cream (page 20) or fill the Blueberry and Lemon Cheese Tart (page 130) with a chocolate sponge and berries. While I've given you some of my tried-and-tested favorite combinations, it's up to you to have fun with them. Baking is all about creativity, and I think tarts and pastries can be some of the most forgiving desserts when changing up the fillings and flavorings. There's no right or wrong, so go with flavors you know you'll love!

hong kong egg tarts

An egg tart, dàntǎ (蛋挞) in Mandarin or dan tat in Cantonese, is a Hong Kong–style custard tart with similarities to a British custard tart. There are two distinct kinds of egg tarts: cookie crust and flakey crust. The cookie crust is reminiscent of a shortcrust, while the flakey crust is puff pastry made from layers of fat and flour. Both are equally delicious but completely different! These egg tarts are my personal favorite; made with a buttery shortbread cookie crust and filled with a sweet and silky egg custard, they will melt in your mouth.

makes 12 (3-inch [8-cm]) egg tarts

special equipment

12 (3-inch [8-cm]) egg tart molds

pastry

1¾ cups (210 g) all-purpose flour, plus more for dusting

2 tbsp (13 g) powdered sugar

½ cup (120 g) unsalted butter, chilled and cubed, plus more for greasing

1 large egg yolk

custard

1⅓ cups (320 ml) whole milk

⅔ cup (130 g) granulated sugar

4 large eggs

1 tsp vanilla extract

To make the pastry, combine the flour, powdered sugar and butter in a large bowl, and use your fingertips to rub the butter into the flour until it resembles sand. Add the egg yolk and mix until a shaggy dough forms. Transfer the dough to a floured surface and knead until a ball forms, then cover with cling wrap and chill for 30 minutes, or until firm.

To line the tart shells, grease the egg tart molds with butter and lightly dust with flour. Once the dough has chilled, divide the dough into twelve equal balls, approximately 1 ounce (30 g) each. Press the dough into your tart molds, and extend the dough 5 mm above the edge of the mold to create a taller tart. This maximizes the amount of custard in each tart. Chill for 1 hour or until firm.

To prepare the custard, heat the milk and sugar in a small saucepan over medium heat for 5 minutes, or until the sugar has dissolved. Meanwhile, in a medium-sized heatproof bowl, combine the eggs and vanilla, and whisk until combined. Slowly pour the steaming milk into the eggs, whisking continuously until well combined. Pour the custard through a fine-meshed sieve into another bowl, or a jug for easy pouring. Set aside until the tart pastry has completely chilled.

To bake the egg tarts, preheat the oven to 320°F (160°C). Remove the chilled tart shells from the fridge and fill the shells to the top with the egg custard. Bake the tarts for 35 minutes, or until the custard is just set. A toothpick inserted in the center of the custard should stand straight without falling.

Remove from the oven and cool for 10 minutes before unmolding. Egg tarts are a lot easier to unmold when warm as they begin to stick after cooling. Be careful, as they will be soft and fragile.

These tarts are best enjoyed warm. Store leftovers in an airtight container in the fridge for up to 3 days. If eating once cooled, reheat the tarts in an oven until warmed through.

raspberry yuzu cream puffs

Cream puffs are always a delight! There is everything to love about these light shells filled with creamy custard, and when topped with a cookie crust they're even better. The cookie crust, or craquelin, gives these an extra sweetness and a crunchy texture that pairs with the yuzu cream and raspberries for the ultimate cream puff. These might look challenging, but all the individual components are easy to put together, and the end result will be completely worth it!

makes 15 cream puffs

yuzu cream

1 batch Pastry Cream (page 20)

1 tbsp (15 ml) yuzu juice

craquelin

⅓ cup (60 g) brown sugar, unpacked

½ cup (60 g) all-purpose flour

¼ cup (60 g) unsalted butter, softened

choux pastry

¼ cup (60 ml) whole milk

¼ cup (60 ml) water

¼ cup (60 g) unsalted butter

¼ tsp salt

1 tsp granulated sugar

½ cup + 2 tsp (65 g) all-purpose flour

2 large eggs

Prepare the yuzu cream as per the Pastry Cream recipe (page 20). Stir in the yuzu juice, cover with cling wrap and place in the fridge for 1 to 2 hours, or until completely chilled.

To prepare the craquelin, combine the brown sugar, flour and butter in a small bowl, and mix until smooth. Place the dough between two sheets of baking paper and roll it out to 3 mm in thickness. Transfer to a baking tray and freeze while preparing the choux pastry.

The craquelin creates a cookie crust over the choux pastry. Not only does this add extra sweetness and texture, but it also evens out the overall shape to create a smooth and rounded pastry.

To prepare the choux pastry, preheat the oven to 375°F (190°C) and line a large baking tray with baking paper. In a small saucepan over medium-high heat, combine the milk, water, butter, salt and sugar, and heat for 5 minutes. When the mixture begins to boil, remove it from the heat and add the flour, mixing vigorously with a wooden spoon until smooth. Return the pan to the heat and flatten the dough to the bottom of the pan. Allow the dough to heat until light crackling can be heard. If you give the pan a shake you'll notice a thin film on the bottom of the pan. This indicates the dough is sufficiently dry and ready to be removed from the heat.

Transfer the dough to the bowl of a stand mixer fitted with a paddle attachment and mix on low speed for 10 minutes to cool. Once cooled to room temperature, add the eggs one at a time, beating in between each addition until smooth and well combined. Transfer the batter to a piping bag fitted with a medium round tip.

Pipe 2-inch (5-cm) round mounds on the lined baking tray, leaving 2 inches (5 cm) in between to prevent them from expanding into each other. Remove the craquelin from the freezer and cut matching 2-inch (5-cm) discs of craquelin using a small cookie cutter. Top each mound of choux dough with a disk of frozen craquelin and bake for 25 to 30 minutes, or until deep golden brown. Do not open the oven during the baking process, as this causes the choux pastries to deflate.

(continued)

raspberry yuzu cream puffs *(continued)*

vanilla whipped cream

1 cup (240 ml) heavy cream

1 tbsp (13 g) granulated sugar

1 tsp vanilla extract

assembly

9 oz (250 g) raspberries, divided

Powdered sugar, for dusting

Freeze-dried raspberry powder, for dusting, optional

Once fully baked, remove from the oven and use a toothpick to poke a hole on the bottom of each pastry to release steam. Place on a wire rack to cool for 30 minutes or until cooled completely.

To make the vanilla whipped cream, combine the cream, sugar and vanilla extract in the bowl of a stand mixer fitted with a whisk attachment and beat on medium speed for 5 minutes, until the cream forms stiff peaks. Transfer the cream to a piping bag fitted with a large French star tip and reserve in the fridge until ready to assemble.

To assemble, reserve 15 raspberries and halve the rest of the raspberries. Once the pastries have cooled, use a sharp serrated knife to slice the tops off. The bottoms of the pastries should form small cup shapes. Transfer the chilled yuzu cream to a piping bag and cut off the tip. Fill each puff one-third of the way with custard, press in a large raspberry, and top with a swirl of vanilla whipped cream. Finish the puffs with the sliced top and decorate with halved raspberries. Sprinkle with powdered sugar and freeze-dried raspberry powder, if using, to finish.

These are best enjoyed the day they're made, as the pastry is still crisp, but they last up to 3 days in an airtight container stored in the fridge.

miso black sesame baked chocolate tart

In comparison to white sesame seeds, black sesame seeds are slightly nuttier, more fragrant and a little more bitter. This in combination with dark chocolate creates a rich and complex flavor that is exactly what you need to elevate a classic chocolate tart. However, this tart doesn't end there . . . a touch of miso in the chocolate custard gives it a kick of salty umami that rounds this stunner off.

makes 1 (9.5-inch [24-cm]) tart

black sesame tart shell

½ cup (70 g) black sesame seeds

1½ cups (180 g) all-purpose flour

2 tbsp (15 g) cocoa powder

2 tbsp (25 g) granulated sugar

⅔ cup (150 g) unsalted butter, chilled, cubed

1 tbsp (15ml) water, iced

miso chocolate custard

1½ cups (360 ml) heavy cream

2 tbsp (35 g) white miso paste

1 tsp vanilla extract

10.5 oz (300 g) dark chocolate, 45% cocoa, finely chopped

2 large eggs

To make the black sesame tart shell, blitz the black sesame seeds in the bowl of a food processor until they form a coarse powder. Add the butter and pulse until the mixture resembles sand. The blitzing won't take very long, so a few pulses will be enough. Finally, add the iced water and pulse until a rough dough forms.

To line the tart, transfer the dough to a clean surface and shape it into a ball. Place the dough on top of a large sheet of baking paper and top with a similar-sized piece of cling wrap. Using a rolling pin, roll the dough out to a 3-mm-thick circle. Flip the dough and remove the piece of baking paper, then carefully transfer the rolled dough to your 9.5-inch (24-cm) tart tin, cling-wrapped side facing up. Using your fingers, carefully press the dough into the tin, then fold and press the overhanging edge of dough against the edge of the tin to trim the edges of the dough. Once the tin is lined, carefully remove the cling wrap and dock the base with a fork. Chill for 1 hour, or until firm.

To bake the tart shell, preheat the oven to 350°F (180°C). Prepare the chilled tart shell for blind baking by lining the inside with baking paper and filling it with baking beans or uncooked rice. Bake the tart for 35 minutes, then remove the beans or rice and bake for a further 5 to 10 minutes, until lightly golden.

Meanwhile, prepare the chocolate custard by combining the cream, miso and vanilla in a small saucepan over medium heat. Place the chopped chocolate in a large heatproof bowl. Heat the cream for 4 minutes, or until steaming, then remove and pour over the chocolate. Cover the bowl with a plate and let sit for 5 to 10 minutes, until the chocolate has completely melted. Stir the chocolate mixture until smooth and set aside for 10 minutes to cool. Once cooled slightly, whisk in the eggs until smooth and pour into the baked tart shell.

Place the tart back into the oven for 15 minutes, or until the edges are set and the center is slightly jiggly. Remove from the oven and cool for 1 hour or until cooled completely.

(continued)

miso black sesame baked chocolate tart *(continued)*

dark chocolate glaze

2 oz (55 g) dark chocolate, 45% cocoa, finely chopped

2 tbsp (30 ml) heavy cream

1 tbsp (15 ml) water

1 tbsp (15 ml) corn syrup or glucose

Flakey salt, for sprinkling

To make the glaze, bring a small saucepan of water to a boil, then reduce to a simmer. In a heatproof bowl slightly larger than the saucepan, combine the chocolate, cream, water and corn syrup. Place the bowl over the saucepan and heat gently for 5 minutes, stirring occasionally, until the chocolate has completely melted. Remove from the heat and pour over the cooled tart. Gently tilt the tart to cover the surface and let sit for 15 minutes.

To create a swirled ganache pattern, place the tart on a turntable. While spinning, use a small offset spatula or spoon to create a swirl, starting at the edge and working inward. Set the tart aside for 1 hour at room temperature to set. Sprinkle with flakey salt before serving.

Enjoy at room temperature for a silky-smooth chocolate tart, or place it in the fridge for a fudgier consistency. Store the tart in an airtight container in the fridge for up to 4 days.

miso caramel banoffee tartlets

This is my twist on the banoffee pie, a classic English pie made with a base of crushed biscuits and butter, caramel sauce, banana and fluffy cream. These tartlets encapsulate everything a classic banoffee is about, but take it to another level. A nutty almond tart shell beats a crushed cookie crust any day, and the miso brings a salty umami depth and flavor to the condensed milk–based caramel. These have been made into tartlets, but the recipe will also fit perfectly in a large tart tin—use what you have!

makes 6 (3-inch [8-cm]) tartlets or 1 (9.5-inch [24-cm]) tart

almond tartlet shells

1 batch Almond Tart Pastry, baked as tartlets (page 15)

caramel

⅔ cup (160 ml) condensed milk

¼ cup (45 g) brown sugar, unpacked

¼ cup (60 ml) treacle or golden syrup

⅓ cup (80 g) unsalted butter

1 tbsp (17 g) white miso paste

whipped cream

1½ cups (360 ml) heavy cream

⅓ cup (35 g) powdered sugar

1 tsp vanilla extract

assembly

2 large ripe bananas, thinly sliced

3.5 oz (100 g) dark chocolate, for shaving

Prepare and bake the tartlet shells as per the Almond Tart Pastry recipe (page 15).

To make the caramel, combine the condensed milk, brown sugar, treacle and butter in a small saucepan over medium heat. Heat, stirring occasionally, for 5 minutes, or until the butter and sugar have completely dissolved. Remove from the heat and stir in the miso until melted. Pour into the baked tartlet shells and chill for 1 hour, or until set.

To make the whipped cream, in the bowl of a stand mixer fitted with a whisk attachment, combine the heavy cream, powdered sugar and vanilla, and whisk on medium-high speed, for 5 minutes, until stiff peaks form.

To assemble the tartlets, arrange the bananas over the chilled caramel. Layer the whipped cream on top of the bananas and use a vegetable peeler or sharp knife to shave the chocolate over the cream.

These tartlets are best enjoyed chilled; reserve the tartlets in the fridge until ready to be served. Store the tartlets in an airtight container in the fridge for up to 3 days.

hojicha white chocolate almond tartlets

Hojicha (焙じ茶), Japanese roasted green tea, is typically made from bancha (番茶), or common tea leaves, and roasted in a porcelain pot over charcoal. This gives the tea leaves a fragrant, caramelized and nutty flavor with a characteristic red-brown color. Unlike matcha, which is very vegetable-forward, hojicha is sweeter and more mellow, a completely different flavor experience. This less polarizing flavor is becoming increasingly popular in desserts and can be found in most Asian groceries! If you haven't tried it, these bittersweet white chocolate tartlets with crunchy almonds and fluffy cream are the perfect way to introduce yourself to your new favorite flavor.

makes 12 (3-inch [8-cm]) tartlets

special euipment

1 St. Honore tip, optional

tartlet shells

Sweet Shortcrust Tart Pastry, baked as tartlets (page 11)

hojicha ganache flling

1 cup (240 ml) heavy cream

15.5 oz (440 g) white chocolate, finely chopped

1 tbsp (15 ml) corn syrup or glucose

2 tbsp (12 g) hojicha powder

vanilla whipped cream

1¾ cups (420 ml) heavy cream

¼ cup (50 g) granulated sugar

2 tsp (10 ml) vanilla extract

assembly

1 cup (143 g) roasted almonds, roughly chopped

Hojicha powder, to dust

Prepare and bake the tartlet shells as per the Sweet Shortcrust Tart Pastry recipe (page 11).

To make the hojicha ganache, heat the cream in a small saucepan over medium heat for 4 minutes, or until steaming. Into a large heatproof bowl, place the chopped chocolate and corn syrup, and sieve over the hojicha powder. Pour the steaming cream over the chocolate, cover with a plate and let sit for 5 to 10 minutes until the chocolate has completely melted. Stir until smooth and set aside.

To assemble the tartlets, arrange the tartlet shells on a baking tray and place a tablespoon of almonds in the base of each shell. Pour in the hojicha ganache and gently tap the tartlets on the counter to smooth the surfaces. Chill for 1 hour, or until set.

Once the ganache has set, make the vanilla whipped cream by combining the cream, sugar and vanilla in the bowl of a stand mixer fitted with a whisk attachment, and beat on medium-high speed for 5 minutes, or until it forms stiff peaks. Transfer the cream to a piping bag fitted with a St. Honore tip, if using, or your tip of choice, and pipe a swirl of cream over the ganache. Scatter each tart with the chopped roasted almonds and dust with hojicha powder.

This tart is best enjoyed chilled; reserve the tart in the fridge until ready to be served. Store the tarts in an airtight container in the fridge for up to 3 days.

mango pancakes

A yum cha classic, Mango Pancakes (芒果班戟) are loved by everybody! Commonly known as mango pancakes, these are a little different than what the name suggests, with the "pancake" having a closer resemblance to a crêpe. I've had my fair share of mango pancakes over the years, and while they may be simple, small things like the thickness of the crêpes, the sweetness of the cream and the freshness of the mango make the biggest difference. As mangoes are the star of the show, make sure you use sweet, ripe mangoes for the best flavor. In Australia, Kensington Pride mangoes are my fruit of choice as they are almost always super sweet. Another great option are Nam Doc Mai mangoes, a variety originating in Thailand. You know your mangoes, so choose your favorites and make some pancakes!

makes 12 pancakes

pancake batter

1 cup (240 ml) whole milk

⅓ cup + 1 tbsp (48 g) all-purpose flour

¼ cup (30 g) cornstarch

2 tbsp (25 g) granulated sugar

3 large eggs

1 tbsp (15 g) unsalted butter, melted

Few drops of yellow food coloring

Vegetable oil, for greasing

filling

2½ cups (600 ml) heavy cream

¾ cup (150 g) granulated sugar

1 tsp vanilla extract

3 large mangoes, peeled and cut into 1.2-inch (3-cm) chunks

To make the pancake batter, combine the milk, flour, cornstarch, sugar, eggs, butter and yellow food coloring in a blender, and pulse until smooth. Pour the batter through a fine-meshed sieve into a large bowl and set it aside.

To make the pancakes, soak a paper towel with vegetable oil and lightly grease a 9.5-inch (24-cm) pan. Heat the greased pan over medium-low heat until warm. Add ¼ cup (60 ml) of batter, or enough to coat the surface of the pan, and swirl the pan to create an even layer. Gently heat the pancake for 2 to 3 minutes, until the surface becomes matte, then remove it from the pan and cool on a baking tray. Repeat with the remaining batter and allow the pancakes to come to room temperature. There is no need to flip them as we want a smooth surface on the outside of the rolled pancakes.

To make the filling, combine the cream, sugar and vanilla in the bowl of a stand mixer fitted with a whisk attachment, and whisk for 5 minutes on medium speed until the cream forms stiff peaks. Cover and place in the fridge until assembly.

To assemble, place a pancake smooth side down on a clean surface and spoon approximately ¼ cup (60 ml) of whipped cream in the center. Top the cream with two cubes of mango and cover with another spoonful of cream. Gently fold in two opposing sides of the pancake, then roll from the bottom up to create a pillow-like shape. Place the rolled pancakes seam side down in a large airtight container and chill for 1 hour to set before serving.

Mango pancakes are best enjoyed chilled; reserve them in the fridge until ready to be served. These are best enjoyed fresh, but can last up to 2 days in the fridge.

blueberry and lemon cheese tart

I first tried this combination of tart and sponge cake during my visit to Japan in a delicious strawberry tart and was surprised by how well the soft sponge cake worked with the crisp tart shell. The combination of fresh fruits, crunchy tart, soft sponge and light cream was a new experience, and I knew I had to create my own version. Blueberries and lemon are a classic combination that pairs exceptionally well with tangy cream cheese for a fresh and fruity tart, perfect for the springtime.

makes 1 (9.5-inch [24-cm]) tart

almond tart shell

Almond Tart Pastry, baked as a large tart (page 15)

sponge cake

6-inch (15-cm) Cotton-Soft Sponge Cake batter (page 19), baked in an 8-inch (20-cm) tin

blueberry jam

4 oz (115 g) blueberries

2 tbsp (25 g) granulated sugar

cream cheese cream

9 oz (250 g) cream cheese, softened

½ cup (100 g) granulated sugar

1 tbsp (15 ml) lemon juice

Zest of ½ lemon

whipped cream

2 cups (480 ml) heavy cream

½ cup (100 g) granulated sugar

1 tsp vanilla extract

assembly

4.5 oz (125 g) blueberries

Lemon thyme, to decorate

Prepare and bake the tart as per the Almond Tart Pastry recipe (page 15). Cool completely.

Prepare the sponge cake batter as per the 6-inch (15-cm) Cotton-Soft Sponge Cake recipe (page 19), but bake for 60 minutes in an 8-inch (20-cm) tin for a flatter cake base. Cool for 1 hour, or until completely cooled, then unmold and slice in half horizontally with a serrated knife.

To make the blueberry jam, combine the blueberries and sugar in a small saucepan over medium heat, stirring occasionally, for 8 to 10 minutes until the blueberries have broken down and thickened. Remove from the heat and cool for 1 hour or until completely cooled.

To make the cream cheese cream, combine the cream cheese, sugar, lemon juice and zest in the bowl of a stand mixer fitted with a paddle attachment, and beat on medium-high speed for 6 minutes, or until light, smooth and creamy. Transfer to a piping bag and set aside in the fridge until assembly time.

To make the whipped cream, combine the cream, sugar and vanilla in the bowl of a stand mixer fitted with a whisk attachment, and whisk on medium-high speed for 5 minutes, or until stiff peaks form. Transfer the cream to a piping bag fitted with a large round tip and place in the fridge until assembly time.

To assemble the tart, place one round of sponge cake in the cooled tart shell and spread the blueberry jam over it. Pipe the cream cheese cream around and over the cake, then top with the other round of sponge cake. Pipe the whipped cream over the whole tart and top with fresh blueberries and sprigs of lemon thyme.

This tart is best enjoyed chilled; reserve the tart in the fridge until it's ready to be served. The tart can be stored in an airtight container in the fridge for up to 3 days.

cloud–like breads

Have you ever bitten into an Asian bread roll and thought to yourself, "How is this so fluffy?!" I remember growing up and wondering why all Asian bakery breads had that characteristic super soft texture and milky taste.

There are a couple of distinct differences between Western and Asian-style bread. Asian-style bread has a higher fat and water ratio to create bread with a super tender crumb, but the secret is in the technique.

After years of trying to recreate the fluffy bread rolls of my dreams, I discovered the tangzhong technique (湯種). Tangzhong is a Chinese word that describes a breadmaking technique originating in Japan in which water and flour are cooked together to create a water roux. This allows the flour to absorb more water, increasing the hydration of the dough and resulting in super soft bread. Once you have this technique mastered, you can make any kind of Asian bakery bread in the comfort of your own home!

While the tangzhong technique might form the basis of this chapter, there is so much more to bread than just the dough. This chapter will take you from Asian bakery essentials like classic Tangzhong Milk Bread (page 134) or Red Bean Buns (page 138) to new and trendy styles of bread like Korean Cream Cheese Garlic Bread (page 141) and Mochi-Dogs (page 150).

tangzhong milk bread

If you are looking for the perfect bread loaf recipe look no further! This slightly sweet, milky bread loaf uses the tangzhong method to create a super soft and tender crumb that stays that way for days. Whether it's served with jam, as a sandwich or simply toasted, this loaf won't disappoint.

makes 1 (9 x 5-inch [22 x 13-cm]) loaf

water roux

3 tbsp (24 g) bread flour

½ cup (120 ml) water

dough

2¾ cups (380 g) bread flour

3 tbsp (37 g) granulated sugar

1 tsp salt

2¼ tsp (7 g) instant dry yeast

⅔ cup milk (160 ml), lukewarm

2 tbsp (30 g) unsalted butter, room temperature

Vegetable oil, for greasing

glaze

1 large egg

1 tbsp (15 ml) whole milk

To make the water roux, combine the flour and water in a small saucepan. Heat over medium heat, stirring constantly, for 4 to 5 minutes, until thickened and semi-translucent. Remove from the heat and transfer to a bowl. Cover with cling wrap and cool for 1 hour, or until room temperature before use.

To make the dough, combine the bread flour, sugar, salt and yeast in the bowl of a stand mixer fitted with a dough hook. Add the cooled roux and lukewarm milk, and mix on medium for 3 minutes, until combined. Ensure the added milk is at 99°F (37°C), the same temperature as your body.

Increase the speed to medium and add the butter. Mix for another 20 to 25 minutes, or until the dough starts to come away from the sides of the bowl; the dough should be able to stretch into a thin sheet without tearing.

Roll the dough into a ball and place it in a large bowl greased with oil. Cover with cling wrap and proof in a warm place for 1 to 2 hours, until doubled in size. Place a mug of hot water in a turned-off oven for the perfect warm and moist proofing environment. The dough is ready when a floured finger inserted in the center creates a hole that doesn't bounce back.

Once proofed, transfer the dough to a floured surface and gently press out the air. Divide the dough into thirds and roll into balls. Using a rolling pin, roll one ball into a long oval. Starting at the short end, roll the dough to form a short cylinder that resembles a Swiss roll or log. Repeat with the remaining two balls, cover with cling wrap and rest for 15 minutes.

Meanwhile, grease a 9 x 5-inch (22 x 13-cm) nonstick loaf tin with oil. Once the dough has rested, turn the log over, seam side up, pointing away from your body, and roll out into a long thin strip 4 inches (10 cm) in width. Starting from a short end, roll the dough to form a short cylinder, place it in the greased tin and repeat with the remaining dough. Loosely cover the tin with cling wrap and place in a warm place for 30 to 60 minutes, until doubled in size. Meanwhile, make the glaze by whisking the egg and milk together.

Preheat the oven to 350°F (180°C) and brush the proofed bread with the glaze. Bake for 20 minutes, or until golden brown. Remove from the oven and cool for 1 hour, or until completely cooled before slicing.

This loaf is best enjoyed the day it's made as it is the softest. Place any remaining bread in an airtight container in the fridge for up to 3 days and gently warm in the microwave or toaster before enjoying!

custard buns

Custard buns or cream pan (クリームパン) are a staple in any Asian bakery! These are usually found in round shapes with a swirl or folded over in half-moon shapes. Either way, these are super delicious, and the combination of soft bread and custard melts in your mouth.

makes 10 buns

dough
1 batch Milk Bun Base (page 23)

pastry cream
1 batch Pastry Cream (page 20)

glaze
1 large egg
1 tbsp (15 ml) whole milk

Prepare the dough as per the Milk Bun Base recipe (page 23).

Prepare the pastry cream as per the Pastry Cream recipe (page 20).

After the first proof, divide the dough into ten equal parts and roll them into balls. Cover with cling wrap and rest for 15 minutes. Roll each ball out to a 4-inch (10-cm) circle. Place a heaped tablespoon of pastry cream in the center of each circle and bring the sides of the dough together. Pinch to seal. Take care not to smear the custard on the parts of the dough that pinch together as it may prevent the bun from sealing properly.

Place the buns on one large or two small baking trays lined with baking paper. Leave 3 inches (8 cm) between the buns to prove; otherwise, they will join as they bake. Loosely cover with cling wrap and place the dough in a warm place for another 30 minutes to 1 hour, or until doubled in size. Meanwhile, make the glaze by whisking the egg and milk together.

Preheat the oven to 375°F (190°C) and brush the proofed bread with the glaze. Transfer the remaining pastry cream into a piping bag and cut the tip to create a small opening. Pipe a swirl of custard on top of each bun and bake for 12 to 15 minutes until golden brown. Cool for 15 minutes before enjoying.

These are best enjoyed the day they're made as they are the softest. Place any remaining bread in an airtight container in the fridge for up to 3 days and gently warm in the microwave or oven before enjoying!

red bean buns

The quintessential Asian-style bread, these buns are filled with sweetened red bean paste also known as anko (餡子), hóng dòu shā (红豆沙) or pat so (팥소). The use of adzuki beans, or red beans, in Asian-style desserts is so common, but it may seem strange if you haven't tried it before. The flavor is sweet and earthy, and pairs incredibly well with a milky bun.

makes 10 buns

red bean paste

1½ cups (300 g) adzuki (red) beans

Water, to cover the beans

1 cup + 2 tbsp (200 g) brown sugar, unpacked

2 tbsp (30 ml) vegetable oil

dough

1 batch Milk Bun Base (page 23)

glaze

1 large egg

1 tbsp (15 ml) whole milk

assembly

Sesame seeds, to decorate

To make the red bean paste, place the adzuki beans in a large pot and add water until the beans are completely submerged. Cover the pot with a lid and bring to a boil. Turn the heat down to medium and cook for 1 hour to 1 hour and 30 minutes, until the beans are easily mashed between your fingers. Drain the beans over a sieve and return them to the pot. Add the brown sugar and cook over medium heat for 5 minutes, or until the sugar has melted and the mixture has thickened. It should be thick enough to hold a line when a utensil is drawn across the base of the pot. Stir in the oil and remove from the heat. Transfer to a shallow dish and cover with cling wrap. Chill for 2 hours to firm up, then roll into ten equal balls.

Prepare the dough as per the Milk Bun Base recipe (page 23).

After the first proof, divide the dough into ten equal parts and roll them into balls. Cover with cling wrap and rest for 15 minutes. Roll each ball out to a 4-inch (10-cm) circle. Place a ball of red bean paste in the center of each circle and bring the sides of the dough together. Pinch to seal.

Place the buns on one large or two small baking trays lined with baking paper. Leave 3 inches (8 cm) between the buns to prove; otherwise, they will join as they bake. Loosely cover with cling wrap and place the buns in a warm place for another 30 minutes to an hour, until doubled in size. Meanwhile, make the glaze by whisking the egg and milk together.

Preheat the oven to 375°F (190°C) and brush the proofed bread with the glaze. Sprinkle with sesame seeds and bake for 12 to 15 minutes until golden brown. Cool for 15 minutes before enjoying.

These are best enjoyed the day they're made as they are the softest. Place any remaining bread in an airtight container in the fridge for up to 3 days and gently warm in the microwave or oven before enjoying!

korean cream cheese garlic bread

I first tried Korean-style garlic bread back when I went on exchange to South Korea, and I was blown away. It's completely different from the classic garlic bread you've grown up eating. It's slightly sweet from the milk bread base and condensed milk, yet full of garlicky buttery goodness, and when paired with a savory cream cheese filling, it's to die for. If anything, the subtle sweetness brings you back for more!

makes 12 buns

dough

1 batch Milk Bun Base (page 23)

cream cheese filling

9 oz (250 g) cream cheese, room temperature

¼ cup (60 ml) heavy cream

1 tsp salt

garlic sauce

1 cup (235 g) salted butter

¼ cup (60 ml) condensed milk

¼ cup (50 g) granulated sugar

12 cloves garlic, minced

¼ cup (6 g) dried parsley

2 large eggs

assembly

¼ cup (22 g) parmesan cheese, grated

1 tbsp (2 g) dried parsley

Prepare the dough as per the Milk Bun Base recipe (page 23).

After the first proof, line one large or two small baking trays with baking paper. Divide the dough into twelve equal parts and roll them into balls. Place the buns on the prepared tray or trays. Cover with cling wrap and proof for 30 minutes to 1 hour, or until doubled in size.

Preheat the oven to 350°F (180°C) and bake for 15 minutes, or until golden brown and cooked through. Cool and cut each bun into six wedges, making sure to not cut the whole way through.

To make the cream cheese filling, combine the cream cheese, cream and salt in a bowl, and mix until well combined. Transfer to a piping bag fitted with a medium-sized round piping tip and pipe into the slices you made in the buns.

To make the garlic sauce, combine the butter, condensed milk, sugar, garlic and parsley in a small saucepan over medium heat. Heat, stirring occasionally, for 4 to 5 minutes, until the butter has just melted. Remove from the heat and transfer to a deep bowl. Whisk in the eggs until well combined.

To bake the garlic bread, preheat the oven to 350°F (180°C). Line a large baking tray with baking paper. Submerge each bun in the garlic sauce, then place on the prepared tray. Sprinkle with the parmesan and parsley, and bake for 15 minutes, or until golden brown. Cool for 5 minutes before enjoying.

These are best enjoyed the day they're made as they are the softest. Place any remaining bread in an airtight container in the fridge for up to 3 days and gently warm in the microwave or oven before enjoying!

fruit sando

These creamy fruit sandwiches, or fruit sando (フルーツサンド), are everywhere in Japan, whether it's a cafe, department store or convenience store. While it might seem strange at first, the super-soft Asian-style bread works perfectly with fruits, custard and cream to create a refreshing sandwich fit for breakfast or a snack.

makes 6 sandwiches

bread

1 loaf Tangzhong Milk Bread (page 134) or store-bought Asian-style milk bread

custard

1 batch Pastry Cream (page 20)

vanilla whipped cream

2½ cups (600 ml) heavy cream

⅓ cup (65 g) granulated sugar

2 tsp (10 ml) vanilla extract

assembly

Assorted seasonal fruits such as strawberries, kiwi or mango, kept whole or in large chunks

Prepare the milk bread as per the Tangzhong Milk Bread recipe (page 134) or use store-bought milk bread, and slice the bread into 0.4-inch (10-mm)-thick slices.

To prepare the filling, make the custard as per the Pastry Cream recipe (page 20). Once cooled, transfer the custard to a piping bag and cut off a medium-sized opening. Reserve in the fridge until assembly.

To make the vanilla whipped cream, combine the cream, sugar and vanilla in the bowl of a stand mixer fitted with a whisk attachment. Beat the cream at medium speed for 5 minutes, or until stiff peaks form. Transfer the cream to a piping bag and cut off a medium-sized opening. Reserve in the fridge until assembly.

To assemble the sandwiches, lay a slice of bread down and pipe a thin layer of vanilla whipped cream across the bread. Lay a line of fruits directly down the diagonal of the bread. Ensure the fruit is placed so that when the sandwich is sliced in half, the fruit's cross-section will be revealed. Pipe a layer of custard on either side of the aligned fruits, fill in any gaps with another layer of whipped cream, and cover with another slice of bread. Repeat with the remaining fruit, cream, custard and bread.

Wrap the sandwiches tightly in cling wrap and chill for 1 hour to set. Once set, remove the cling wrap and slice off the crusts with a sharp serrated knife. Then cut down the diagonal of the sandwich to reveal the fruity cross-section.

These are best enjoyed the day they're made as the bread is still soft. Place any remaining sandwiches in an airtight container in the fridge for up to 2 days.

tangzhong cinnamon rolls

A good cinnamon roll is everyone's weak spot. The tangzhong base gives these rolls an extra pillowy softness that lasts for days, and when they're swirled with cinnamon brown sugar and a slathering of tangy cream cheese frosting, how can anyone resist?!

makes 9 large or 12 small buns

dough

1 batch Milk Bun Base (page 23)

cinnamon filling

⅔ cup (120 g) brown sugar, unpacked

¼ cup (60 g) unsalted butter, room temperature

2 tbsp (16 g) ground cinnamon

cream cheese frosting

4 oz (115 g) cream cheese, room temperature

¼ cup (60 g) unsalted butter, room temperature

½ cup (50 g) powdered sugar

1 tsp vanilla extract

Prepare the dough as per the Milk Bun Base recipe (page 23) through the first proof.

To make the cinnamon filling, combine the brown sugar, butter and cinnamon in the bowl of a stand mixer fitted with a whisk attachment. Whip on medium speed for 5 minutes, or until light and fluffy.

To form the cinnamon rolls, prepare a 9 x 13–inch (22 x 33–cm) rectangular tin. After the first proof of the milk bun dough, transfer the dough to a floured surface and gently press out the air. Roll out into a 12 x 16–inch (30 x 40–cm) rectangle, the shorter end facing your body. Spread the cinnamon filling in a thin and even layer across the dough, then tightly roll the dough away from you to create a swirled log. Using a sharp knife, slice the log into nine or twelve equal pieces and space them evenly in the prepared tin. For large, fluffy buns, slice the dough into nine portions; for smaller buns slice into twelve. Loosely cover with cling wrap and place the dough in a warm place for 30 minutes to 1 hour until doubled in size.

Preheat the oven to 340°F (170°C) and bake the twelve buns for 20 to 25 minutes, or the nine buns for 25 to 30 minutes, until golden brown. Cool slightly.

While the rolls are cooling, make the frosting. In the bowl of a stand mixer fitted with a paddle attachment, combine the cream cheese and butter, and beat on medium-high for 4 minutes, or until smooth. Add the powdered sugar and vanilla, and continue to beat for 3 minutes, or until light and fluffy.

Ice the cinnamon rolls as soon as the frosting is ready and the rolls are slightly warm. This allows the rolls to absorb some frosting for extra moisture and sweetness.

These are best enjoyed the day they're made as they are the softest. Place any remaining bread in an airtight container in the fridge for up to 3 days and gently warm in the microwave or oven before enjoying.

ube custard donuts

These ube-filled donuts are my take on Bombolini, Italian sweet yeast donuts rolled in sugar with a custard filling. Instead of a classic Italian pastry cream (crema pasticcera), these are filled with a Filipino-inspired ube-flavored custard, giving these donuts a nutty, vanilla-like flavor that pairs perfectly with the fluffy fried dough.

makes 6 donuts

donut dough

1⅓ cups (190 g) bread flour

1 tsp (4 g) instant dry yeast

2 tbsp (25 g) granulated sugar

¼ tsp salt

1 large egg

⅓ cup (80 ml) whole milk, lukewarm

2 tbsp (30 g) unsalted butter, softened

ube custard

2 large egg yolks

2 tbsp (25 g) granulated sugar

2 tbsp (40 g) ube halaya

½ tsp ube extract

1 tbsp (7 g) cornstarch

½ cup (120 ml) whole milk

assembly

Vegetable oil, for frying

Granulated sugar, for rolling

To make the donut dough, combine the flour, yeast, sugar and salt in the bowl of a stand mixer fitted with a dough hook. Add the egg and lukewarm (99°F [37°C]) milk, and mix on medium for 4 minutes, or until well combined.

Add the butter and continue to beat for 15 to 20 minutes, or until the dough starts to come away from the sides of the bowl (it should be able to stretch into a thin sheet without tearing). Roll the dough into a ball and place it in a large bowl greased with oil. Cover with cling wrap and proof in a warm place for 1 to 2 hours, until doubled in size. The dough is ready when a floured finger inserted in the center creates a hole that doesn't bounce back.

Meanwhile, make the ube custard. Combine the egg yolks, sugar, ube halaya, ube extract and cornstarch in a medium-sized heatproof bowl. In a small saucepan, heat the milk for 4 minutes, or until steaming. Slowly pour the hot milk into the ube mixture, whisking continuously. Return the mixture to the pan over low heat and whisk for 4 to 5 minutes, until thickened. It should be thick enough to hold a line when a utensil is drawn across the base of the saucepan. Remove from the heat and transfer to a bowl. Cover with cling wrap and chill for 1 hour, or until completely cooled.

Once the dough has proofed, line a baking tray with baking paper. Transfer the dough to a floured surface and gently press out the air. Divide the dough into six equal portions and roll into balls. Place on the prepared tray and cover with cling wrap. Place the tray in a warm place for 30 minutes to 1 hour, until doubled in size. The donuts are ready to be fried if your finger leaves an indent in the dough with a light spring back. Cut the baking paper so that each ball is on its own square of baking paper.

Heat a pot of vegetable oil to 340°F (170°C). Carefully pick up each donut by the corners of its baking paper and place it into the preheated pot of oil. Fry for 2 to 3 minutes on each side until golden brown, removing the baking paper after 30 seconds. Drain on a wire rack or paper towel and repeat with the remaining donuts, three at a time to avoid overcrowding. Place the sugar in a small bowl. While the donuts are still warm, toss them in the sugar to coat. Cool for 1 hour, or until cooled completely.

Once the donuts and ube custard have cooled completely, transfer the ube custard to a piping bag fitted with a medium-sized round or bismark tip. Using a chopstick, create a hole on the top of each donut and insert the piping tip into the donut to fill. These donuts are best consumed on the day they are made; enjoy them fresh!

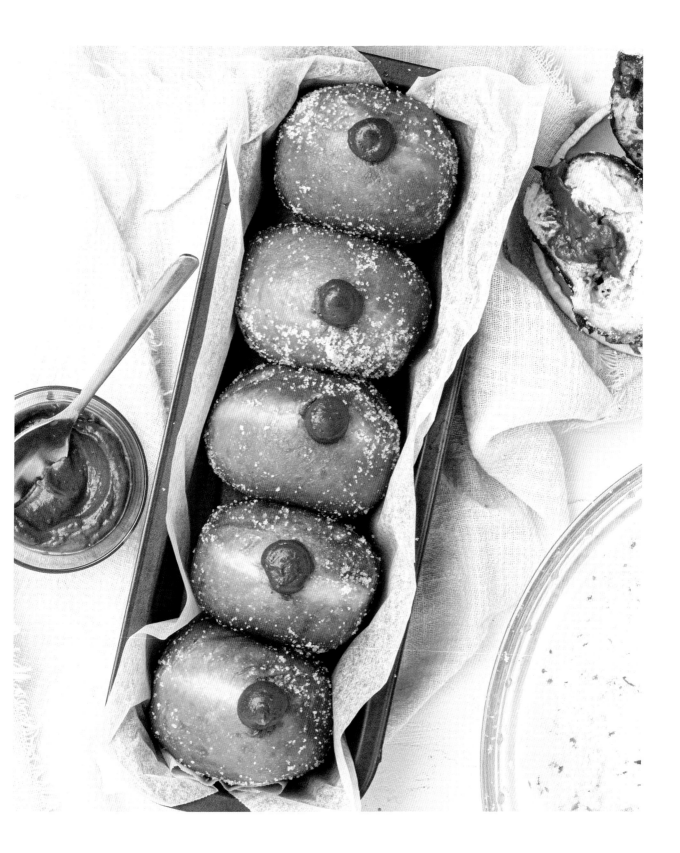

strawberries and cream melon pan

Melon pan (メロンパン) is a classic Japanese bread made of a simple bread dough base and a buttery cookie crust, but why is it called "melon pan"? Although the origins of this bread are unclear, it is thought that the patterned cookie crust resembles the skin of a melon, and "pan" (パン) means bread in Japanese! These days there are so many variations, from green melon flavored buns to buns filled with ice cream. This strawberry version adds light vanilla cream and tangy strawberries to the freshly baked soft and crunchy bun for a refreshing and contrasting texture. Feel free to play around with the fillings to create your own version.

makes 10 buns

cookie topping

¼ cup (60 g) unsalted butter, softened

1½ cups (300 g) granulated sugar, divided

1 large egg

1½ cups (175 g) cake flour

½ tsp baking powder

1 tbsp (6 g) freeze-dried strawberry powder, optional

dough

1 batch Milk Bun Base (page 23)

vanilla whipped cream

2½ cups (600 ml) heavy cream

½ cup (100 g) granulated sugar

1 tsp vanilla extract

9 oz (250 g) strawberries, trimmed and sliced

To make the cookie topping, combine the softened butter and ½ cup (100 g) of sugar in the bowl of a stand mixer fitted with a paddle attachment and beat on medium speed until light and fluffy. Add the egg and beat until combined. Sieve in the flour, baking powder and freeze-dried strawberry powder, if using, and beat until just combined. Wrap the cookie dough in cling wrap and chill for 1 hour, or until it's completely chilled.

Prepare the dough as per the Milk Bun Base recipe (page 23). After the first proof, divide the dough into ten equal parts and roll them into balls. Place 1 cup (200 g) of sugar in a shallow bowl. Remove the cookie dough from the fridge and divide it into ten equal portions. Place each cookie dough portion between two pieces of baking paper and roll into a 2-mm-thick round. Remove the baking paper and top each dough ball in cookie dough. Roll the cookie dough side in the granulated sugar and score a criss-cross pattern into the cookie dough with the back of a knife.

Place the buns on one large or two small baking trays lined with baking paper. Leave 3 inches (8 cm) between the buns so they don't join together as they bake. Loosely cover with cling wrap and place the buns in a warm place for another 30 minutes to 1 hour, until doubled in size.

Preheat the oven to 350°F (180°C) and bake for 13 to 15 minutes until lightly golden brown. Cool for 1 hour on the counter or until completely cooled.

To make the vanilla whipped cream, combine the cream, sugar and vanilla in the bowl of a stand mixer fitted with a whisk attachment. Whisk on medium-high speed for 5 minutes, or until stiff peaks form, and transfer to a piping bag fitted with a large star tip.

Once the buns have cooled, slice each bun horizontally down the middle, making sure not to cut the whole way through. Fill with whipped cream and slices of fresh strawberries. These are best enjoyed the day they're made as they are the softest. Fill just before enjoying. Place any remaining unfilled bread in an airtight container in the fridge for up to 3 days and gently warm in the oven before enjoying.

mochi-dogs

Sweet and crunchy Korean-style hotdogs have been taking over the internet. Everyone is in love with the crunchy coating, dusting of sugar and crazy sauces. These trending hotdogs originated in a store called Myungrang Hotdog (명랑핫도그), which specializes in hotdogs made with rice flour. I've recreated them to produce a hotdog with a uniquely chewy, yet fluffy texture that is so moreish! There are many possible fillings, from stretchy mozzarella to chewy rice cakes. I've gone with a classic cheesy hotdog, but play around with them to suit your tastes!

makes 4 hotdogs

special equipment

4 wooden skewers

dough

1 cup + 2 tbsp (160 g) bread flour

⅓ cup (43 g) glutinous rice flour

2 tsp (8 g) granulated sugar

1½ tsp (4 g) instant dry yeast

½ tsp salt

½ cup (120 ml) water, lukewarm

¼ cup (60 ml) whole milk, lukewarm

assembly

Vegetable oil, for frying

3 cups (170 g) panko bread-crumbs, for rolling

2 hotdogs, halved widthwise

4 sticks low-moisture mozzarella cheese

1 cup (200 g) granulated sugar, for rolling

Ketchup, for serving

Honey mustard, for serving

To make the dough, combine the bread flour, glutinous rice flour, sugar, yeast and salt in a large shallow dish. Add the water and milk, and mix to combine. Ensure the added water and milk are at 99°F (37°C), the same temperature as your body. Loosely cover with cling wrap and let the dough rise in a warm place for 30 minutes to 1 hour until doubled in size.

To prepare the mochi-dogs, place the panko breadcrumbs on a plate. Uncover the dough. Slide the halved hotdogs followed by the cheese onto the wooden skewers, so that the hotdog and cheese are stacked vertically on top of one another, and dip the prepared skewers in the dough. Twist the skewers in a single direction until they are completely covered in dough. The dough will be sticky and hard to handle. If you are having trouble, use your hands to stretch a thin layer of dough over the hotdog. Transfer the coated hotdogs to the panko and roll to coat.

To fry, pour the vegetable oil into a large deep frypan and heat over medium heat until 350°F (180°C). If you don't have a thermometer, the oil is ready if a small piece of white bread turns golden when added. Carefully place two to three mochi-dogs in the oil at a time and fry for 4 to 6 minutes, turning constantly, until golden brown. Meanwhile, place the sugar on a plate. Remove the fried mochi-dogs from the oil, drain on a wire rack or paper towel, and roll in the sugar. Drizzle with ketchup and honey mustard to serve.

These mochi-dogs are best consumed on the day they are made; enjoy them fresh!

creamy treats

This chapter is all about creamy, delicious goodness. I've covered the whole spectrum from puddings to popsicles.

If I had to choose one food to eat for the rest of my life it would be ice cream. There is something so addictive about that smooth texture, and lucky for us it's not that hard to make at home.

Homemade ice cream is creamier than commercially made ice cream due to a gentler churning process. This may make the ice cream firmer straight out of the freezer, but it results in a mouthfeel unlike anything you can get from the supermarket!

While homemade, churned ice cream is incredible, I understand that most households won't have an ice cream machine on hand . . . and I've got you covered. There's a mix of churned and no-churn ice creams in this chapter so you can choose what works for you. And even if you have an ice cream machine, it's nice to make an easy no-churn ice cream once in a while!

The other creamy desserts in this chapter are all twists on classics, like a Cantonese-style Mango and Passionfruit Sago (page 157) or a French Earl Grey Crème Brûlée (page 161). Little adaptations give these classics an extra boost to create delicious Asian-inspired desserts.

yuzu blueberry swirl ice cream

This yuzu ice cream is one of my absolute favorite recipes. The unique, tangy fragrance of yuzu is the ideal flavor for a creamy dessert and is a popular flavor in Japan. The blueberry swirl adds a sweet touch, but feel free to change it up with other fruits like raspberry or strawberry, or even a cream cheese swirl for a yuzu cheesecake ice cream. I like to use xanthan gum as it helps stabilize the ice cream base and give it a creamier texture; however, if you can't get your hands on some, feel free to leave it out. It'll be equally delicious!

makes 1 pint (480 ml) ice cream

ice cream base

4 large egg yolks

1 cup (200 g) granulated sugar

1 tsp xanthan gum, optional

¼ cup (60 ml) yuzu juice

1 tbsp (15 ml) lemon juice

Zest of 1 lemon

2 cups (480 ml) whole milk

1 cup (240 ml) heavy cream

blueberry swirl

4 oz (115 g) blueberries

3 tbsp (38 g) granulated sugar

To make the ice cream base, whisk the egg yolks, sugar, xanthan gum, if using, yuzu juice, lemon juice and zest together in a heatproof mixing bowl until well combined. In a small saucepan over medium heat, combine the milk and cream, and heat for 4 minutes, or until steaming. Slowly pour the steaming milk into the egg yolk mixture, whisking continuously until well combined. Return the ice cream base to the saucepan and whisk over medium heat for 4 to 5 minutes, until slightly thickened. The mixture should be thick enough to coat the back of a spoon.

Remove from the heat and transfer to a bowl. Cover with cling wrap and chill overnight, or for a minimum of 4 hours before churning.

To make the blueberry swirl, combine the blueberries and sugar in a small saucepan over medium heat. Heat the blueberries, stirring occasionally for 5 to 6 minutes, until the blueberries have broken down and thickened slightly. Remove from the heat, cover and chill until completely cooled.

Once the ice cream base has chilled completely, churn in your ice cream maker according to the manufacturer's instructions.

Transfer the churned ice cream to an airtight container and fold in the blueberry swirl. Cover and place in the freezer for a minimum of 4 hours, or until chilled.

Allow the ice cream to sit at room temperature for 15 minutes before scooping and enjoying. The texture of homemade ice cream is best when consumed within 1 to 2 weeks.

mango and passionfruit sago

Traditional Chinese sago is made with small pearls of bouncy tapioca, and served in a coconut-based broth for a sweet dessert soup. It's a simple and delicious classic Cantonese dessert perfect for summer, or a refreshing palate cleanser typically found at the end of a yum cha feast. To be honest, I'm not sure if I go to yum cha for the food or desserts like egg tarts, tofu pudding, mango pudding, mango pancakes and sago; there are too many options to choose from. This mango sago, however, is levels above any kind you'll get at yum cha. With smooth mango coconut puree and fresh passionfruit to cut through the creaminess, you'll keep coming back for more.

makes 4 sagos

½ cup (75 g) sago pearls

2 large mangoes, peeled and diced, divided

¾ cup (180 ml) coconut milk

¼ cup (50 g) granulated sugar

Whole milk, to serve

Pulp of 4 passionfruit, to serve

To cook the sago, bring a large pot of water to a boil over high heat. Add the sago, reduce the heat to medium and cook for 8 minutes, or until the sago is transparent with an opaque center. Turn off the heat and cover for 10 minutes, or until the sago is fully transparent. Drain and transfer to a large bowl of iced water.

Meanwhile, in a blender, combine half the mangoes, coconut milk and sugar, and blitz until smooth.

To serve, divide the sago and mango coconut puree between 4 cups. Top with fresh milk, passionfruit pulp and the remaining mangoes.

Enjoy immediately or store the mango coconut puree and sago together in an airtight container for up to 2 days. Top with passionfruit and milk before serving.

lychee panna cotta with vanilla strawberries

You know you've made a great panna cotta when it has a good wobble, and that comes down to the perfect ratio of cream and gelatin. This panna cotta is smooth and silky with just enough gelatin to hold it together. Lychees have a sweet and delicate flavor that compliments the silky texture of panna cotta, and when served with vanilla strawberries they create a sophisticated yet easy dessert that is bound to impress.

makes 6 panna cotte

special equipment

6 (4.25-oz [120-ml]) ramekins or dariole molds

panna cotta

3 tbsp (45 g) cold water

3 tsp (9 g) powdered gelatin

1 cup (240 ml) lychee syrup, from a can of lychees

2 cups (480 ml) heavy cream

¼ cup (50 g) granulated sugar

Vegetable oil, for greasing

vanilla strawberries and lychees

9 oz (250 g) strawberries, trimmed and quartered

¼ cup (50 g) granulated sugar

1 tsp vanilla bean paste

3.5 oz (100 g) lychees, fresh or canned, pitted and quartered

To make the panna cotta, add the cold water to a small bowl and sprinkle over the gelatin, whisk to combine and set aside to bloom for 3 minutes. In a medium saucepan, combine the bloomed gelatin, lychee syrup, cream and sugar. Heat over low, stirring occasionally, for 4 minutes, or until the sugar and gelatin have completely dissolved. To check whether everything has dissolved, rub the panna cotta mixture between your fingers. If the mixture is smooth without any graininess, it's ready.

Lightly grease six ramekins with vegetable oil. Pour the panna cotta mixture into the prepared ramekins and cool to room temperature. Cover each with cling wrap and chill overnight, or for a minimum of 6 hours, until set.

Meanwhile, in a large bowl, combine the strawberries, sugar and vanilla bean paste, and toss to combine. Stir in the lychees, cover with cling wrap and place in the fridge to macerate while the panna cotte set.

There are two serving options: in the ramekin or unmolded on a plate. If serving the panna cotte in the ramekins, simply remove the cling wrap and top with vanilla strawberries and lychees.

If unmolding the panna cotte, submerge each ramekin in a bowl of hot water for 10 seconds. Remove from the water, cover with an inverted plate and flip the plate and ramekin over so the plate faces the right way up. Carefully lift the ramekin to reveal the panna cotta. If the panna cotta doesn't slide out, give the mold a few firm taps with a wooden spoon. Top the unmolded panna cotte with vanilla strawberries and lychees to serve.

Store any unserved panna cotte, covered or in an airtight container, in the fridge for up to 3 days. Top with vanilla strawberries and lychees before serving.

earl grey crème brûlée

Crème brûlée is a classic French custard dessert topped with a layer of crunchy caramelized sugar. This recipe infuses the milk and cream with Earl Grey tea to create a delicious and fragrant bergamot-flavored custard. It's hard to find someone who doesn't love a creamy baked custard and crunchy caramel!

makes 6 crème brûlées

special equipment

6 (3.4-oz [97-g]) ramekins

1 blowtorch, optional

earl grey crème brûlée

3 Earl Grey tea bags

1¼ cups (300 ml) heavy cream

¾ cup (180 ml) whole milk

5 large egg yolks

⅓ cup (65 g) granulated sugar

2 tsp (10 ml) vanilla extract

6 tbsp (80 g) superfine sugar, for torching

To infuse the cream, place the tea bags, cream and milk in a medium saucepan. Bring to a boil and remove from the heat. Cover and allow the tea to infuse at room temperature for at least 2 hours, or in the fridge overnight for a deeper flavor.

To prepare the crème brûlée, preheat the oven to 320°F (160°C) and place six medium ramekins in a baking pan. Remove the tea bags from the cream, pour the infused cream into a small saucepan, and heat over medium heat for 4 minutes, or until steaming. Meanwhile, in a large heatproof bowl, combine the egg yolks, sugar and vanilla, and whisk to combine. Slowly pour the steaming milk into the egg yolk mixture, whisking continuously until well combined.

Pour the custard mixture through a fine-meshed sieve into another bowl, or a jug for easy pouring. Then divide the custard between the prepared ramekins. Fill the baking tray with 0.8 inches (20 mm) of boiling water and bake for 30 minutes, or until the custard is just set. The sides should be set, while the center remains jiggly. Remove from the oven and cool to room temperature. Cover each ramekin with cling wrap and chill for a minimum of 6 hours.

To serve, remove the ramekins from the fridge and sprinkle over 1 tablespoon (13 g) of superfine sugar on each ramekin. With a blowtorch, if using, torch the sugar until golden brown and caramelized. If you don't have a blowtorch, place the ramekins sprinkled with sugar on a tray directly under a broiler preheated at high. Keep an eye on them and remove them as soon as they are caramelized. Serve immediately.

Store these before caramelizing, covered or in an airtight container in the fridge for up to 3 days. Remove and caramelize before serving.

matcha ice cream

If there was one ice cream flavor I could eat for the rest of my life it would be matcha. The balance between earthy matcha and the sweet creamy custard base keeps you coming back for more! As green tea is the dominant flavor, I would recommend using a high-grade culinary or ceremonial grade matcha powder for a bright flavor without a bitter aftertaste, but feel free to increase or decrease the amount used to match your favorite intensity. I like to use xanthan gum as it helps stabilize the ice cream base and give it a creamier texture; however, if you can't get your hands on some, feel free to leave it out. It'll be equally as delicious!

makes 1 pint (480 ml) ice cream

¾ cup (150 g) granulated sugar

3 tbsp (18 g) matcha powder

1 tsp xanthan gum, optional

2 cups (480 ml) whole milk

1 cup (240 ml) heavy cream

To make the ice cream, combine the sugar, matcha powder and xanthan gum, if using, in a medium bowl and whisk to combine. In a medium saucepan over medium heat, combine the milk and cream, and heat for 5 minutes, or until steaming. Remove from the heat and whisk in the mixture of sugar, matcha powder and xanthan gum, if using, until smooth. Return the saucepan to the heat and continue to heat the cream, whisking continuously, until slightly thickened. The mixture should be thick enough to coat the back of a spoon.

Remove from heat and transfer to a bowl. Cover with cling wrap and chill overnight, or for a minimum of 4 hours before churning.

Once the ice cream base has chilled completely, churn in your ice cream maker according to the manufacturer's instructions.

Transfer the churned ice cream to an airtight container, cover and place in the freezer for a minimum of 4 hours, or until chilled.

Allow the ice cream to sit at room temperature for 15 minutes before scooping and enjoying. The texture of homemade ice cream is best when consumed within 1 to 2 weeks.

no-churn thai milk tea ice cream

Thai milk tea (ชาเย็น) is a creamy Ceylon tea with hints of spices like orange blossom water, star anise and tamarind seed. Known for its bright orange color and spiced taste, it's a sweet and delicious tea perfect as a base for ice cream. Thai milk tea is typically sweetened with condensed milk, so all you need are four ingredients to make the creamiest spiced ice cream, no mixer required!

makes 1 pint (480 ml) ice cream

2½ cups (600 ml) heavy cream

½ cup (40 g) Thai tea mix

1 cup (240 ml) condensed milk

1 tsp vanilla extract

To make the ice cream, combine the cream and Thai tea mix in a medium saucepan over medium heat. Bring to a boil, remove from the heat and set aside to cool. Cover and chill for a minimum of 6 hours to allow the cream to infuse.

Once the cream has chilled, remove it from the fridge and pour it through a fine-meshed sieve or cheesecloth into the bowl of a stand mixer fitted with a whisk attachment. Whisk the cream on medium speed for 5 minutes until it forms stiff peaks. Add the condensed milk and vanilla, and fold to combine.

Transfer the ice cream mixture to an airtight container. Cover and place in the freezer for a minimum of 4 hours, or until chilled.

Allow the ice cream to sit at room temperature for 15 minutes before scooping and enjoying. The texture of homemade ice cream is best when consumed within 1 to 2 weeks.

brown sugar boba popsicles

Boba has become an iconic Asian drink worldwide, and Taiwan's signature brown sugar boba is among the best kinds. The boba is cooked in thick brown sugar syrup and served with fresh milk for a chewy and delicious sugary drink. It wasn't long ago that brown sugar popsicles were released in supermarkets and took Asian communities around the world by storm. I mean, what's not to love about frozen bubble tea? This is my recreation of that delicious treat: soft and chewy brown sugar pearls in creamy ice cream. Make sure you use glutinous rice flour rather than tapioca starch in the boba, as that's what keeps them soft despite being frozen!

makes 10 popsicles

special equipment

10-cavity popsicle mold

soft boba

¾ cup (100 g) glutinous rice flour

⅓ cup (60 g) brown sugar, unpacked

¼ cup (60 ml) water, boiling

Cornstarch, for dusting

syrup

⅓ cup (60 g) brown sugar, unpacked

1 tbsp (15 ml) water

1 tsp cornstarch

milk tea ice cream base

2 cups (480 ml) heavy cream

¼ cup (60 ml) condensed milk

To make the soft boba, combine the glutinous rice flour, brown sugar and boiling water, and mix to form a rough dough. Transfer the dough to a surface dusted with cornstarch and knead until smooth. Divide the dough into three equal portions and roll each portion into a log 10 mm wide. Working with one log at a time, cut off 5-mm pieces. Roll each piece into a ball and dust in cornstarch to prevent them from sticking to each other. While you are working on one log, keep the other logs covered with cling wrap to prevent them from drying out.

To cook the boba, bring a large pot of water to a boil. Add the boba and stir to prevent them from sticking to the bottom of the pot. Boil for 3 to 5 minutes, until the boba floats to the surface of the water, then drain.

Meanwhile, prepare the syrup by combining the brown sugar, water and cornstarch in a small saucepan. Once the boba has been cooked and drained, add it to the pan. Heat the boba and syrup ingredients over medium heat for 4 to 5 minutes, until the sugar has dissolved and thickened. Transfer to a bowl and cool for 1 hour, or until completely cooled.

To make the ice cream base, combine the cream and condensed milk in the bowl of a stand mixer fitted with a whisk attachment, and whisk on medium speed for 4 minutes, or until the mixture forms soft peaks.

To assemble, transfer 1 tablespoon (4 g) of brown sugar boba to each cavity of a ten-cavity popsicle mold and use a spoon to run some of the sugar syrup along the walls of the mold. Carefully fill each cavity halfway with the ice cream base, add another tablespoon of brown sugar boba and fill to the top with the remaining ice cream base. Insert a popsicle stick into each cavity and place the popsicles in the freezer to set overnight, or for a minimum of 6 hours.

Unmold the popsicles and allow them to sit out at room temperature for 10 minutes before consuming. These are best enjoyed within 2 to 3 days as the boba will firm up if stored in the freezer for too long.

asian ingredients glossary

The following is a list of all Asian ingredients used in this book. Many may be familiar and others might be completely new. Take these flavor profiles and add them to your own desserts to create your very own versions.

Adzuki bean: Adzuki beans, also known as red beans, are grown across East Asia and are well-known for their application in confectionery. The beans are most commonly boiled, then mashed or ground into a paste. The paste can then be sweetened and used in traditional sweets like rice cakes or used as a filling for bread and cakes. The flavor is earthy and delicious on its own or paired with cream or other earthy flavors like matcha, nuts and sesame.

Boba: Boba, or pearls, are balls of tapioca starch that are cooked to a chewy texture. Boba can refer to the drinks served with tapioca pearls, or the pearls themselves. Originating in Taiwan, boba is typically served with milk tea and a thick straw to slurp up the deliciously chewy pearls as you drink.

Glutinous rice flour: Also known as sweet rice flour, glutinous rice flour is made from ground long- or short-grain glutinous rice. The most common brand available in Asian groceries is the Thai Erawan Brand, in green packaging, made from long-grain rice. All mochi recipes in this book were developed with long-grain glutinous rice flour as it is the easiest to access. However, there is also a Japanese variety called mochiko (餅粉) made from short-grain glutinous rice, which has a chewier and less sticky texture. Both long- and short-grain varieties will work to create delicious mochi, with slight differences in texture.

Hojicha: Hojicha (焙じ茶), also known as Japanese roasted green tea, originated when unsellable bancha (番茶), late harvest tea leaves, were roasted in a porcelain pot over charcoal. This roasting process creates a new tea flavor that is caramelized, nutty and fragrant with a sweeter flavor. Served as whole tea leaves or ground into a powder, this red-brown tea is gaining traction across the world for its delicious and versatile flavor. Its earthy flavor works great in sweet desserts like ganaches, caramels and rich cakes.

Lychee: Well-known and loved across the world, lychee is a sweet and slightly floral fruit originating in Southeastern China. The fruit found inside the red skin is sweet and juicy, with a slightly acidic touch. Now found all across the world, the flavor works amazingly in delicate desserts like light sponges, custards and puddings.

Matcha: Matcha (抹茶) is made from steamed and dried green tea leaves that are stone-ground to form a fine powder. Its origins date back to Zen Buddhist monks during the Tang Dynasty in China. The tea leaves and processes were taken back to Japan, where they were refined and perfected. Now the finest matcha is grown and crafted in Japan, where the vegetable-forward, slightly bitter taste is known and loved. The grassiness of matcha pairs well with sweet or creamy desserts like white chocolate or ice cream to create a delicious bittersweet flavor.

Miso: Miso (みそ or 味噌) is a traditional paste made by fermenting soybeans with salt and koji, a fungus. Originating as a method to keep food for longer periods of time during the warmer months in ancient China, miso was introduced and popularized in Japan, where it has now become an integral part of the culture. This savory, salty paste is typically used to make soups or add flavor to marinades and sauces, and its application in desserts has been increasing over the past couple of years. The fermented bean paste adds an umami kick and depth of flavor that contrasts with the sweetness of many desserts to create a sweet-salty combination. Try adding miso to sweet desserts made with chocolate and caramel for a unique twist.

Pandan: Pandan, also known as a screwpine tree, is a tropical plant grown in Southeast Asia. The tree grows long and spiky leaves that are used in Southeast Asian cooking because of their unique fragrance and aroma. Found commonly in Asian groceries dried, frozen, ground or as an extract, the leaves can be used to wrap savory dishes, cooked in soups, or used in sweets and baked goods like cakes. The flavor is grassy with hints of vanilla and coconut, and pairs well with lightly flavored sweets like rice cakes, sponges, jellies and mousses. Try it with coconut for a delicious and fragrant flavor combination.

Sesame: Sesame seeds are used across the world in all kinds of cuisines, with applications in sweet and savory dishes like halva or hummus. On the other hand, black sesame seeds are more common in Asian cuisine, appearing in the fillings of Japanese and Korean rice cakes and Chinese glutinous rice dumplings. Their fragrant and nutty nature makes them very versatile and works in most fruity, sweet and creamy situations.

Thai tea: Thai tea is a Ceylon tea infused with spices like orange blossom water, star anise, cloves and tamarind seed. It can be served hot or cold, but is most commonly served iced with sweetened condensed milk. Known for its bright orange color and sweet creaminess, Thai iced tea, or cha yen (ชาเย็น), is loved worldwide and its spiced flavor and vibrant color is perfect in desserts.

Ube: Ube is a root vegetable originating in the Philippines, known for its bright purple color and sweet vanilla-like flavor. Used in both savory and sweet cooking, the flavor is more commonly used in confectionery, prepared with condensed milk to create a jam called "ube halaya." Ube halaya can be served on its own or in Filipino sweets like halo-halo, a layered dessert made with shaved ice. With ube's rise in popularity these days, its sweet, slightly nutty flavor is used in all sorts of desserts from cakes to donuts.

Yuzu: Yuzu (柚子) is a yellow-green citrus originating in East Asia. It has a thick lumpy skin, floral aroma and sour, bitter flesh. The flavor is often compared to a combination of lemon and grapefruit; however, it is prized because of its floral fragrance. Commonly used in Japanese cooking to make salts, sauces and marmalades, yuzu is now found all over the world in desserts. Its unique flavor profile adds a zing to cut through sweetness, or a light perfumed fruitiness to creams and mousses.

acknowledgments

To my parents, thank you for your continuous support no matter what decision I make. It was thanks to you both that I was able to pursue a career that I love and live the life I am living. Thank you for putting up with my carelessness and craziness. I wouldn't have made it this far without you both!

To my editor, Aïcha, thank you for presenting me with the opportunity to write this book and allowing me to share my love for baking and Asian flavors. Your support and guidance has helped this book come together with ease.

To Adriano Zumbo, thank you for your words of wisdom. You've been my idol and inspiration on this journey! Thank you for setting aside time to contribute to this book. It truly means a lot.

To Isabel, my sister, thank you for all your emotional support. You're always there when I'm going through a disaster and I just need someone there. I can guarantee 50 percent of this book was created while Facetiming you, and it wouldn't be the same without that. Thanks for keeping me company during my late-night photoshoots and long days of writing.

To Miho, thank you for being you. You've been with me through all my highs and lows, and without you, I wouldn't be where I am now. Thank you for picking me up when I've fallen off the path of life and for being there during the best times. Love you bestie!

To Uki, thanks for sticking with me. I can't appreciate your bluntness enough, whether it's toward my desserts or life in general, and your undying support in whatever I do gets me through everything. Love you!

To my Zumbo family, Zak, Kylie, Kristie, Pearly, Megan, Jeff, Rachel, Simon and Kimberly! Getting to know you all through season two of *Zumbo's Just Desserts* was the biggest blessing. You are all so incredibly talented and hardworking, and it's been such a journey watching all of us grow together. While we might all be in different parts of Australia, I'm so glad we keep in touch and bond over the one thing that brought us all together: desserts!

about the author

Catherine Zhang is a Chinese-Australian recipe developer and pastry chef located in Sydney, Australia.

At nineteen she appeared on season two of Netflix's reality television show *Zumbo's Just Desserts*, hosted by Australian pastry chef Adriano Zumbo and British cook and writer Rachel Khoo. After competing with nine other home cooks, she emerged as champion.

She graduated from the University of Sydney with a degree in food and nutrition science, and began a career as a pastry chef, only to pursue a career in recipe development and food media soon after.

Catherine is now working as a recipe developer while running her blog zhangcatherine.com and other online platforms where she regularly uploads dessert and baking recipes inspired by her Asian background.

index